W9-AQN-668

Girls Write Now: Two Decades of True Stories from Young Female Voices offers a brave and timely portrait of life as a teenage girl in the United States over the past twenty years. They're working part-time jobs to make ends meet, deciding to wear a hijab to school, sharing a first kiss, coming out to their parents, confronting violence and bullying, and immigrating to a new country while holding on to their heritage. Through it all, these young writers tackle issues of race, gender, poverty, sex, education, politics, family, and friendship. Together their narratives capture indelible snapshots of the past and lay bare hopes, insecurities, and wisdom for the future.

Interwoven is advice from great women writers—Roxane Gay, Francine Prose, Chimamanda Ngozi Adichie, Zadie Smith, Mia Alvar, Janet Mock, Lena Dunham, Gloria Steinem, Quiara Alegría Hudes, Alice Walker—offering guidance to a young reader about where she's been and where she might go. Inspiring and informative, *Girls Write Now* belongs in every school, library, and home, adding much-needed and long-overdue perspectives on what it is to be young in America.

More praise for Girls Write Now:

"Warning: there is so much heart, intensity, guts, and sheer talent in these pages, you're going to need to remind yourself to breathe."

—LYNN MELNICK

"Each story here is a reminder that we build writers by not only believing that they have the talent and spirit it takes to write, but also by showing them how our very voices can influence the world."

—LISA LUCAS

"Seeing these brilliant and driven young women take on the world through words gives me so much hope for the future, both of television and the world."

—JENNI KONNER

"Frankly, I'm jealous of the young women who have Girls Write Now as a community and source of encouragement, and I wish I'd had that as a young book nerd, writing alone in my bedroom. Even now as an established writer, I'm so grateful for the hope it gives me."

—MORGAN PARKER

"Electric, filled with more ideas, energy, and power than all the light bulbs in the Empire State Building. If these girls are the future, which of course they are, the future is glorious."

—EMMA STRAUB

GIRLS WRITE NOW

Published by Tin House Books, Portland, Oregon and Brooklyn, New York.

Distributed by W. W. Norton and Company.

Library of Congress Cataloging-in-Publication Data is available.

First US Edition
Printed in the USA
Interior design by Diane Chonette
www.tinhouse.com

GIRLS WRITE NOW

Two decades of true stories
from young female voices

 TIN HOUSE BOOKS / Portland, Oregon & Brooklyn, New York

Table of Contents

ROXANE GAY

FRANCINE PROSE

CHIMAMANDA NGOZI ADICHIE

ZADIE SMITH

MIA ALVAR

JANET MOCK

LENA DUNHAM

GLORIA STEINEM

QUIARA ALEGRÍA HUDES

ALICE WALKER

"Everyone has a voice. It's just a question of finding the courage to use it, and the first step in finding the courage is knowing that no matter who you are or how quiet you think your voice is, your voice matters. You're never going to please everyone with what you say, but you don't have to worry about that. You only have to satisfy yourself to start with, and I think, with that kind of acceptance, you can begin to use your voice. Regardless of any insecurities you feel, you have to have an innate confidence in yourself and your voice because if you don't believe in your voice, then no one else is going to listen."

-- ROXANE GAY --

Dear Kanye, January 14th

BY DANNI GREEN, 2012

January 14, 2012 7:45 pm

Dear Kanye,

Nine days ago I called financial offices of the colleges I applied to. Told them I had to submit my FAFSA without parental information. Told them Shawn won't give me his information, and my mother and I have tried. Told them how Shawn raises his voice, shows his ignorance, and shouts like he's Otis Day. How he calls me stupid. Says I shouldn't be trying to get money from the government. Every time my mom and I try.

Each college said my parents are married and Shawn lives in the house so they couldn't help me. They told me I was in *a tough situation*. They told me I was in a tough situation like I didn't know that. Like I don't see the lives of the people I live with and how content, like a snake, has opened its mouth and swallowed their lives whole. My brother Robert is jobless. Almost thirty. Has an Associate's degree and no idea what to do with his life. My sister Jessica is sleeping with the man she loves and isn't her husband. She just got laid off. Has four children and no more Food Stamps. And her rent has to be paid. My brother Darius made a house out of my Grandfather's room to avoid everything that's on the outside of his door. My younger brother Philip has taken the Geometry Regents three times.

Cuts classes. Smokes weed and wonders what he'll do with his life. My mother. Had she gone to UCLA would be a doctor right now. The closest Aunt Carla has gotten to being an actress is watching the Academy Awards every year. She flips the pages of her celebrity tabloids looking for herself.

Who am I supposed to look up to? Who is supposed to show me how I can make my dreams real?

I'm watching Jon Sands and Adam Falkner live at The Bowery Poetry Club. But I'm sitting in my computer chair looking at them on a screen. Seeing them makes me want to pull the pretty stars out the sky. Rip open my chest and stuff them in. Because I want to be pretty. On the inside. And I'm hoping stolen stars can shine away whatever's in me trying to kill the person I can be if I were only not Here.

Adam was my English teacher. Last summer I bought Jon Sands's book. I know this guy. Like, had conversations with this guy. Like went to this guy's workshops. If they are not made of better stuff than me, like stars, then why are they where I want to be and I am not?

I'm not in a tough situation, Kanye. But if I don't get out of the house on Wyckoff Street I will be, but it'll be My Life. It'll be a husband I don't love, an affair to make me feel alive, a checking account with a zero balance, a job that'll brand me Good Enough, and children whose faces ask *What's for dinner?*

Currently it's 7:54. The 14th day of 2012. A Saturday. But it feels like 2011 and 2010 and '09 and '08 and '07 and '06, and every year when I felt I was absolved of any good thing in me the second I walked through the front door of my house. Barriers between the days are crumbling and morphing 24 hours into one long minute.

There is too much contempt in my soul to have a life like the ones I see daily. My family has redefined happiness to make their lives mean something. Since the second semester of tenth grade I worked my ass off to get As. I lost sleep to write essays, didn't hang out with friends to do homework.

But it's slowly sinking in. There isn't an escape from what dirties the dishes and puts the dust between the floorboards of my house. Not living your dreams is a sickness. My parents are carriers. It is in my plasma waiting to infect my cells. And sometimes I cry like I'm terminally ill. The tears tumbling down to my shirt is evidence that I'm dying. Because everything has just gotten so hard. Like breathing. Like having faith in myself. Like believing I won't stay Here. College was supposed to get me out of Here.

Now I'm too full of fear that I'm going to be My Family. I've seen the way their muscles fold, how their joints crack. I feel that what's in Them is seeping into me. At times I ask myself, *Who am I kidding thinking that I'll be different? That I'll do something with my life?*

Adam is playing the piano. Jon Sands just read a poem. I like it. The crowd clapped. I want someone to clap for me. To be proud of me. Tell me *Good Job.* So I could stop thinking I'm such a failure. Because I strived for college but can't pay and will likely defer a year, and I'll see my friends leave and I will stay. Jon Sands is up in front of people. A mic before him. Performing poems. All I want to do is write poems. Touch someone with my poems. I want someone to like them. What am I doing with my life that I'm not on stage. That I'm not There? If I were There I wouldn't know another hungry night, I wouldn't be scared to pray. I wouldn't wake up feeling so weak. I'd be doing something with my life. I'd . . . I'd . . .

Did you ever ask yourself, Kanye, *what am I doing with my life that I'm not There?* If you did. What was your answer?

DANNI GREEN was born in New York, NY. She attended Academy for Young Writers in Brooklyn, NY, and Lewis and Clark College in Portland, OR.

Adhan

BY MISBAH AWAN, 2016

The sweetest sound I have ever heard is the sound of *adhan*—Muslim call to prayer—especially in countries with large Muslim populations. Hearing it on the streets is a completely different matter than hearing it inside a mosque, because the location already implies thinking of worship. However, when I hear it while walking down the streets, I not only find myself relaxed and at peace but also begin to really see the synchronized unity among Muslims. I found this sense of peace in Pakistan when I was about eight years old. As soon as the *adhan* went off from a high point in the city, it spread across miles, and the imagery around me transformed. Coming from America to visit the motherland became an entirely new experience with that sweet sound. The shops and restaurants and rides came to a slow pause. If there was not a masjid nearby, people prayed inside their shops or outside on the streets.

I am able to feel similar comfort in the bustling community in New York City, though. Although the *adhan* does not reach across neighborhoods, inside the masjid I feel safe. Usually the masjids, unfortunately, imitate the socioeconomic situations in our communities. Often, they are socially dominated by Arabs in between prayers and gatherings. It becomes cliquey. However, once the *mu'adhin*—the person who calls people toward prayer—intones, "The prayer is due, the prayer is due," everyone—young or old, black or white, poor or rich—lines up behind the *Imam* in rows and begins to pray.

The feeling of comfort I get from that sound, and these communities, has led me to download a Prayer App on my phone to respond to my religious duty. I plan to take it with me to college, because prayer gives me the time to pause life—either to mentally process it or simply to step out of it for the moment.

I am currently going through a metamorphosis; however, the call to prayer is part of my personal revolution. I want to continue to feel for it and want it.

MISBAH AWAN was born in Parkistan and was raised in Queens, NY. She attended The Young Women's Leadership School of Astoria, in Queens, NY, and Bard College in Annandale-on-Hudson, NY.

Step

BY ANGELICA ROZZA, 2014

On my street, growing up, it took under thirty-two steps to walk straight
to any store. After school, as I passed my friends walking together, or with
their parents—knowing my mother was home in bed—I counted the steps
it took to get to each store so I would know how fast it would take to get
home. Back in my apartment, after putting away bags of whatever I pur-
chased for my mother, I would read stories to her that I had written. Trying
to get her to smile, I used theatrical gestures and my best storytelling voice.
Growing up with a mother who has bipolar disorder, no day was a straight
or level line. But even on days I was needed at home and wasn't able to join
my friends, no day went by without my writing stories.

I wrote at a desk by a window that faced the stores on the street.
Picking up my mother's prescriptions at the pharmacy took thirty-one
steps. The market took twenty-four. When my mother was not able to
work and things got rough with money, we had to barter with the land-
lord by buying him food as payment for rent. In the market, I weighed
bananas and apples, and whatever fruit cost the least. I learned how to
be observant and resourceful, to take charge, and to value caring for
someone else. Though I didn't realize it at the time, all those steps I took
on my street have shaped me into who I am today.

Learning to pay attention to details and cues that signaled my mother's needs allowed me to transfer this awareness to my writing. I tried to tap into the heart of each character I created. Every day, I wrote pages about different characters, creating adventures and stories about their lives. This gave me a sense of connection to a world outside my home life that I often didn't feel growing up.

But there were times growing up when I enjoyed my mother's company. During the summer of my first year of high school, the last summer with my mom's Honda, we drove into Queens. Although we didn't have much to say to one another, we walked in and out of small antique shops, both falling in love with antique picture frames and salt-and-pepper shakers.

As the day progressed and the sun boiled above us, her irritability began to surface. I knew that the best thing to do was leave before she had a full-blown episode. Instead, she walked into a hole-in-the-wall bookshop. The place was crowded with thick books on uneven, wooden shelves. Greeting cards and bookmarks collected dust on the main desk in front of the brass cash register.

My mom told me to look around. The mustiness of old books gave me an instant headache. I decided to pick up the closest book with the most interesting cover. A hardcover, with a purple slip, caught my attention. I ripped it out from a tightly packed shelf as quickly as I could without pulling the whole shelf down. My mother grabbed it from my hands and the cashier rang it up. Twelve dollars. Before I could escape the embarrassment and snatch it back from the cashier with a swift excuse, my mother began fishing through her pocket. First came the crumpled five-dollar bill. Then came the handful of change. And without as much as a blink of the eye, my mother counted. The cashier waited for every quarter, dime, nickel, and penny, and then dumped the handful of change into the brass register that clanked with every coin. The book was mine. As we left the store, with the book tucked under my arm, my mother turned to smile at me. Without much thought, I grabbed her hand and crossed the street with her to the car. Those were steps I walked with joy.

My mother is the woman who taught me to stand on my own two feet. And for every time the silence grows too loud between us, I'll remember that she spent her last handful of coins on me in that bookstore. I'll remember that she has always tried her best to make me smile. I've learned to cherish my time with her, because for every bad day, there was a good day that made it all worth it again. And despite all the rough patches her disorder created, her faith in me, and my passion for writing, will always motivate me to move forward.

ANGELICA ROZZA was born in Brooklyn, NY. She attended Long Island City High School in Queens, NY, and SUNY New Paltz in New Paltz, NY.

Kiss Me

BY CLIO CONTOGENIS, 2010

I pull the door up against my back and as it clicks, the party's light is cut off and we are left in darkness, the sound of our breathing amplified by the bathroom's tiled walls. I let my hand slide to the doorknob, brush it past the light switch. No. I like the dark, the mystery. My head stops spinning in its cool comfort.

I catch her outline in the mirror. The few flecks of light left with us reflect on its surface to form a nimbus of gold around her head, distinguishing the few electrified hairs standing upright away from her face, but not her features.

We're still laughing too hard, overflowing with our secret, because we're so clever, we're doing it here where they can't see. Where not even we can see. Our dizzied giggles make me wonder if we're actually going to do this. We're stalling, but I'm thrilled with expectation. Our hands explore the air nervously, excitedly, and our fingertips touch. We weave them and press our palms together, and my breath comes faster because this is happening. A hook slips under my rib cage and pulls upward, leaving me feeling strangled, nauseous, exhilarated. My head is rushing and it's not just the alcohol.

I don't want to kiss her.

What does it mean that I'm dying to? I'm curious, just exploring, but I *want* to. My giggles are no longer from hilarity because my breath is simply shaking them out. I can't stop; we're both laughing because this is so funny and then it's not funny anymore. Or at least we're not laughing. I don't know who decided the silence, but I do know that I see the white expanse of her neck stretch upward against the mirror's glint and I slide my hand onto it, along the smooth curve of her chin and under the earring she was afraid of losing earlier tonight. We haven't moved but suddenly we're kissing and her tongue is soft against mine. I close my eyes, but nothing changes. It's so dark and then we're pulling apart. I let my breath out, relieved.

But it was too short and I want nothing more than to fall into that kiss again. Sarah was right. Girls are better at it.

Now we're joking again as we stagger into the light and tell James and Michael that they missed it. We're horrified when they don't believe us. *But we did, we did!* We did it just for them, didn't we? To frustrate them because they couldn't see? *Do it again,* they say, *now. Then maybe we'll believe you.* No, we're not that easy—we'll do it, but only in the bathroom again, and we link hands and push through their protests back into our darkness. James tells Michael not to worry. *It's OK. We can just open the door,* he says, and I hear him but I don't tell her. Because I don't want her to stop, I want the door closed behind us again, my hand slipping through the smoothness of her hair and her arms around my shoulder blades.

Then the dark is there and there's no laughter this time. I know they're coming, but I don't care. *Kiss me,* she whispers, and I need no urging and when light bursts in through the door and James screeches in delighted surprise, we barely stop. *We told you so,* and then our lips touch again and mine smile against hers.

CLIO CONTOGENIS grew up in Hudson Heights, NY. She attended Stuyvesant High School in New York, NY, and Yale University in New Haven, CT.

Hijabi or Jihadi?

BY ROMAISSAA BENZIZOUNE, 2016

It's kind of awkward to "share" a religion with a band of killers who bomb capital cities and shoot up holiday parties in their free time.

It's not the frustrating awkwardness of falling on the school steps, or even the tragic awkwardness of wearing a denim-on-denim ensemble.

It's the kind of awkward where I actually ran away upon seeing a stack of newspapers on the sidewalk that described ISIS's attacks on the Stade de France. To be fair, my phone had died and I was hopelessly lost; away from the *Washington Post* seemed as good a direction as any.

Terrorism is a hard thing to outrun.

Hardly a moment has passed since then, and already there is a new group of people to grieve for even closer to home. A new collection of xenophobic Republican statements that I must make a point to debunk before the next horror hits.

You have to understand that my initial thought following these terror attacks was probably similar to yours: *Oh my God, these crazy fanatical Muslim terrorists.*

My second thought was more like one of those dreadful realizations you have after you wake up: *Wait, I am Muslim.*

How do I forget something like that for even a minute, you ask? I mean that's my whole thing, right? Like, hello, loud hijabi over here, victim of general American ignorance, self-appointed educator of both students and teachers—in a *gifted* school, no less—but of all misconceptions, the fabulous star in her own sitcom life, etc.

Could it be possible that I, Hijabi in Plain Sight, am a secret Islamophobe?

I know that terrorism has no color or creed; that the word "Islam" itself means "peace"; that the Qur'an reads, "Whoever kills an innocent, it is as if he has killed all mankind." And that ISIS has not only violated this basic tenet of Islam but dozens more. (What kind of Muslim bombs a mosque? You're not even supposed to wear your shoes in a mosque. I've seen someone get the stink eye for reading the Qur'an too loudly.)

Despite all these facts, every time I hear the name of my own religion—and it's usually coming from the mouth of some politician who garbles the "s" into an omnipotent, multisyllabic "z"—I cringe. The Arabic meaning of the word bites at me like a personal mockery.

Peace. That's my religion. Literally. There are only so many times I can try and explain what the word *jihad* really means. There are only so many times I can try to explain the difference between a helpless refugee fleeing ISIS and an actual member of ISIS. Between beheading people and putting it up on YouTube and actually practicing Islam.

Like all Americans, I have processed the Islam/terrorist association. Unlike most Americans, however, I am at once the target audience and the monster to be feared.

This is an unpleasant state of being.

For the first few days after the Paris attacks, I kept myself in the dark. But there was no escaping the tragedy. When I tried to look up sites on which to illegally re-watch *The Mindy Project*, I found myself staring at the tiny black ribbon on Google's homepage. I tried to find humor in an episode of *Saturday Night Live* only to be A) met with a Paris-related intro, and B) reminded that Kristen Wiig was no longer part of the cast.

And when I went back to school the Monday after Paris, an exceptionally nice girl came up to me and hugged me.

I felt relief at first—*she understands*—followed by a twinge of annoyance.

Now, there are many reasons why I would like to be hugged. Surviving a weekend in rural Pennsylvania with no Wi-Fi. Consistently dropping the ball in gym class in front of a certain someone. Enduring the SAT (again) at a testing site where the sole hallway decoration was a laminated Tupac quote—something about dreams—peeling off the wall.

Note that international terrorism is not on that list.

The girl was being nice. But even sympathy propels me further and further away from normal, from the possibility that being American and being Muslim could someday overlap.

I am seventeen years old.

It is crushing to think about spending an entire life shape-shifting and explaining and overcompensating in a desperate attempt to prove that I'm okay. That I too am American. An entire life watching people watching me and wondering what they think, even though it is entirely possible that they don't care at all. My grief, my anxiety, my sense of alienation and obligation cannot be resolved with a brief "we stand with Paris" cold open.

This column was supposed to be funny. It was supposed to be about gym class. But after the Paris attacks the plans changed. After San Bernardino they changed again.

What happens tomorrow?

ROMAISSAA BENZIZOUNE was born in Queens, NY. She attended Hunter College High School and New York University in New York, NY.

Mott Street between Houston and Prince

BY SAMANTHA CARLIN, 2002

We're looking at $338 sandals in a Mott Street boutique and I say *one day I'll write a book that will let me buy them without blinking.* And then I wonder why I care so much, because across the street there's a four-hundred-year-old church with a four-hundred-year-old graveyard that is molding in the most meticulous natural patterns I've ever seen. And inside, my posture is perfect against the ninety-degree angles of the pews and I see him praying like he means it and I wonder where his faith comes from and why he lets out an earnest cry—a grown man giving in to feeling.

He catches me looking and my eyes flick away to the rays of color disguised as windows, and suddenly I notice the silence stinging like long-awaited relaxation, or maybe death, or maybe it's just a pure silence I've never heard before, but by the time I look to see him again, he is gone.

I'm outside again and the sun is merely a jester when it should be king. I look over my shoulder and I see him walking, sandwiched between two friends, and he looks over his shoulder at me. I flick my eyes away to the café with the line out the door and the boutiques I'll shop in when I have the money, and I wonder why I care so much.

SAMANTHA CARLIN was born in Englewood, NJ, and grew up in Hillsdale, NJ. She attended Pasack Valley High School in Hillsdale, NJ, and Barnard College in New York, NY.

Model Minority Girl

BY MAGGIE WANG, 2017

Being a first-generation immigrant is often aligned with the struggle of balancing two different cultures—the impossible battle of trying to fit in and conform to both cultures while molding a separate identity. While culture is inherited, it is cultivated through one's environment. My inheritance of Asian and American identities has been shaped and molded to fit the environment I am in—a conflicting resolution to my sense of self.

As a Flushing native, I grew up surrounded by Asians and Asian Americans. My parents fit in perfectly with the boisterous crowds rushing past the test-prep centers and bubble tea shops—a homogenous mesh of Chinese dialects and yellow skin. However, even in such a nondiverse community, there were still small differences that my parents draw pride from. As an East Asian, I was always told that I was simply superior. My parents claim another level of superiority, often looking down on other Asian immigrants who are not as well-acclimated to American ways, have "country" dialects, or are less educated. For them, becoming Americanized was not the goal, but rather adapting and becoming successful in a foreign country. For them, having an Asian American daughter meant that I had an advantage over regular Asian immigrants and that I could be the perfect, obedient child.

My parents' ideals were reflected in elementary and middle school, where "Asian American" was synonymous with the best kind of conformity. My fellow classmates in the "alpha" class and I saw ourselves through an elitist lens, as "the model minority"—superior because of our intersectionality, as if being Asian American was a superpower that separated us from everyone else. We looked down at the "FOBs"—the immigrants with the broken English and homemade lunches we constantly sought to distinguish ourselves from. While it was bad to be an immigrant, it was also bad to be Americanized and called a "Twinkie": yellow on the outside, white on the inside. We began to try to top one another with the most ethnic experience we could regale. We shared the pains of Tiger Moms and forced lessons, be it violin, ballet, or Chinese folk dance, and the pressures of upholding the standard of the perfect Asian child.

We wanted to be exotic because we, with our perfect English scores and Lunchables, were still trying to figure out how to balance this duality of cultures. We did not know what it meant to be an Asian American, afraid we had conformed too much to the American lifestyle and had lost sight of our Asian culture and traditions. I clung to what my parents expected of me because I thought their expectations reflected what a true Asian should be. So, I committed to violin, even when my fingers became callused; committed to Chinese folk dance, even when my teacher grabbed my stiff, inflexible legs and forced me down; and committed myself to being the perfect Asian daughter with an English tongue, even when the only words I was allowed to say were: "Yes, I will do better."

When I entered Hunter College High School, I learned that not only did I not know what it meant to be Asian but I also did not understand what it meant to be American. It used to be easy to be an Asian American. But at Hunter, there are no immigrants with broken English, and the desire to prove that we belong in this elitist, Upper East Side school was suffocating. For the first time, I wanted someone to call me a Twinkie. Among the Asian Americans, there were clear distinctions of popularity based on the ability to conform with American culture—TV shows, neighborhoods, stores, and music—nothing I had experienced before. I was afraid of being grouped with the girls who watched Korean dramas, who tried to emulate Japanese culture, or who tried to be the best in class. I did not want to be categorized in the subgroups for Asian girls, as if they were the only identities we could ever possess—never equal to the popular kids and their boundless identities. I felt like I had to prove myself every time I went to school, as if what I wore, where I went for lunch, and what kind of music I listened to meant that I was more than my skin. I grew ashamed of my Asian identity. Ashamed that every time I looked in the mirror, I could see why that white girl in my class confused me with my friend, even after being in the same class for a year.

This suffocating desire to conform over the years has made me realize that there is no guide to being an Asian American. No matter how many ways I try to distinguish myself, to perform for other people's perception of me, no one can tell me who I am. Being Asian American is my blood and birthright. I am not your Twinkie, your lesser, your copycat. I am not your Model Minority girl.

MAGGIE WANG was born in Queens, NY. She attended Hunter College High School in New York, NY, and Binghamton University in Binghamton, NY.

Hummingbird

BY ROCIO CUEVAS, 2009

I am a hummingbird. I have bright blue-and-green feathers. I am trapped in a cage and confused as to why I can't get out.

I am a pair of Payless sneakers sitting on the shelf watching everyone glancing at me and walking away. I am all these things. But I am NOT precise. Nor am I definite.

ROCIO CUEVAS was born in Brooklyn, NY. She attended EBC High School for Public Service and New York University in New York, NY.

Life in Odd Numbers

BY MARQUISELE MERCEDES, 2015

Three

The hours on a bus from Albany to the City. It is twenty-one dollars for a
ticket, not including the train ride uptown into spray-painted subway signs
and late-night service delays. Your sister rolls her black duffle bag through
the melted snow on the cracked pavement, ignoring the guys who stand at
the corner of Gun Hill Road and Burke Avenue. There is one there who
proclaims his love on a regular basis—both directly and indirectly. Yet she
has no time. Franderis moves too fast for his feet and his mind, leaving him
to choke on her icy dust. So does she. The cold air constricts her asthmatic
airways and makes her wheeze. When she arrives at one in the morning—
brown cheeks stained with pink, black hair plastered to her sweaty forehead—she kicks the front door with her boots.

Five

The number of twenty-dollar bills your mom spares to gift you on your
birthday. They are in separate envelopes; the silver-and-black striped
enclosures are embedded with generic phrases like "it's your special day"
with too many exclamation points. Her fine brown fingers cradle the
sides of your head and your bashful "thank you" is lost to the sound of

her smacking kisses on your frizzy hair. The custom-made ice cream cake is at the center of the table in front of you, butchered by a hot knife, oozing dulce de leche. It lies beside a present you have yet to open. You wonder, in dread, how much it cost, but then remember you were born during income tax season. Your stomach stops its churning.

Seven

The charms on your bracelet that tinkle like small wind chimes when you move too enthusiastically. You remember how you got each and every single one. The retro sunglasses for the white-sand beach of Punta Cana. The crescent moon clip to match the ink behind your ear. The dangling butterfly and heart, both imbued with feelings of "forever." Each one inspires deep, vigorous love—the kind that rushes through you like rapids and threatens to swallow you up when you're lonely. They constantly remind you that you are not—lonely, that is—but you find yourself pushing into the corner of your room, making friends with the loose threads on your stuffed cow. They've come to grips with the fact that it's just who you are.

Nine

The grade you slipped on a slope peppered with spikes. You are left with shredded insides and weak legs and a broken mind and it is hard to get back the breath that is knocked out of you. You start to let your mom stroke your hair when the pain is too much and reluctantly admit that you like it when you are left alone and she is at work. At the bottom of the slope is a dark pit and you are in it for three years. At first, you are too broken to try to climb out. You get comfortable on the mold-covered ground, ignore your sour stench, and eat what can stay down. But when you finally hear them calling your name, you start to claw at the walls. Your brain blocks the climb out, but you suck in the fresh air greedily, hear them cheer despite the fact that everything is different and you are not perfect. And when your feet continue to dangle over the edge of the pit, they do their best to help you not fall in again.

Eleven

The hour you were born. Your mom says you and your sister were clean and shiny. Your father is too late to cut your umbilical cord, but that is okay because he doesn't fit in with the rest of the story anyway. Your sister wonders why you are so much lighter than she is, but she still loves you. You can see it in an old, unfocused picture probably taken by Mom. Franderis holds you like she's supposed to, and the gap between her two front teeth is brilliant. And in your bones, you know they will stay with you always.

MARQUISELE MERCEDES was born in New York, NY. She attended the Dewitt Clinton High School in the Bronx, NY, and Hunter College in New York, NY.

Four Eyes

BY KIARA KERINA-RENDINA, 2013

I have my father's eyes, eyes that are the color of an oak tree. Eyes that are pulled down by invisible strings on the outermost corners. Eyes that gravity pulls down like a hunched back. Eyes that have seen so much but understand so little. Eyes that share love and experiences that will last forever through our memories.

His eyes stayed awake on school nights, burning from fatigue, whispering "one last page" as their lids brushed together. His eyes watched pages fade to darkness as psychedelic plots floated in the space between the cornea and the optic nerve. My eyes stay alert from five to ten, skimming lines of documents and watching television in a tempest of letters and images. My eyes rest at night, drooping low from overuse, like withering orchids.

His eyes skimmed parents' bookshelves for mature novels, famished for something of substance. His eyes found themselves devouring *The Godfather* and *The Drifters* as a small herbivore would devour a plant. My eyes spin through Barnes & Noble in a frenzy, searching for the final book of a seemingly endless A Song of Ice and Fire series. My eyes swim through sheets of paper in a lake filled with unraveling subplots and dying characters.

His eyes watched blood seep out of two holes where a glass bottle has sliced a leg swimming in a quarry. His eyes watched as she nibbled at these fissures that didn't seem so bad until they needed eight stitches to be sewn back together again. My eyes watched a small thumb stick itself too close to the door when it slammed and promptly turn the color of the fingernail to that of a plum. My eyes felt tears well up and overflow quickly like a bathtub faucet that has been left alone and forgotten.

His eyes watched as term papers about the legalization of anything less than conservative were stamped into a crisp, blank sheet. His eyes watched those term papers receive grades from an angry teacher, as fruitless as an apple tree in a desert. My eyes strain over a computer screen that blinks white and black in a pattern of vowels and consonants, shooting pages out of an eager printer. My eyes watch anxiously as a classmate hands them back, grades as satisfying and filling as a warm cup of tea being sipped in a soft place.

His eyes watched pizza dough thrown by his father fly higher than they could see, feeling a head tilting backwards to watch. His eyes watched that pizza come down as gracefully as a ballerina from a bluebird lift. My eyes watch an older version of the same patriarch as he instructs hands to fill ravioli with a mixture of cheese and spices with the same perfect amount each time. My eyes watch as small bits of filling ooze out when the ravioli is flipped over and squeezed to be sealed and readied for mealtime.

Our eyes saw the bleached pillars of Pompeii rise high, fighting other tourists for an inch of shade. Our eyes saw each other stagger up a mountain, sweaty and silent as we pretended that our feet weren't hurting. Our eyes stayed up until early hours, watching old movies and new releases and everything in between. Our eyes see each other.

KIARA KERINA-RENDINA was born in New York, NY. She attended Millennium Brooklyn High School in Brooklyn, NY, and Sarah Lawrence College in Yonkers, NY.

House Keys

BY IEMI HERNANDEZ-KIM, 2004

"What about our bras with the wires?" a blonde girl with a European accent asked in my gym class. Everyone giggled.

"And what if we have a ring in our vagina?" a Colombian girl with hair dyed red and green and dressed in chains and black punk clothes asked. She had a joking yet serious attitude.

All that the gym teacher could say was, "I don't know."

Recently, a letter was handed out that said metal detectors will be randomly put in our school. Everyone took the letter and cursed at it.

Then today, when the metal detectors were put in the main entrance, only a handful knew since most students use the side entrances.

People talked about cell phones being taken away, along with iPods and some knives. Here's the funny part—a while ago a security guard got slashed in the face with a house key after she pulled a girl's hair and got into a fight. House keys are one of the few things that won't be taken away.

So, while metal detectors are being put in schools, people will find other things to use as weapons.

What will they throw at us when this time comes?

IEMI HERNANDEZ-KIM was born in Mexico City, Mexico. She attended Edward R. Murrow High School in Brooklyn, NY, and New York University's Tisch School of the Arts in New York, NY.

A Walk through My Life

BY LAUREN MELENDEZ, 2014

You open the dark brown door, all busted up. Walk through a lobby with dirty, worn-out walls, black floor . . . dried gum, sticky footprints. Five floors, no elevators. Just stairs.

Every Tuesday they do apartment inspections. To make sure we're actually living there. Just me, my mom, my twin sister, and my brother—no extras or you get kicked out.

Cameras on the first two doors. Watch for bad neighbors doing drugs and weed. Grinning in dark hoodies and torn jeans; suspicious sounds: arguing, yelling. Gunshots in the park.

Sometimes clanking radiators sizzle. But sometimes they don't give us heat. When there's no heat, there's no hot water, just the smell of wet paint and weed, and I can't take a shower.

I don't know why we got bed bugs. They came out of nowhere and it took forever to get them exterminated. We flipped our beds, they sprayed. We stayed with my grandparents.

Soon we'll get out of that hellhole. Start a new chapter, get stuff out of storage. Mom will have her spices and she'll make brownies again. Just because she can.

LAUREN MELENDEZ was born in New York, NY. She attended Marta Valle High School in New York, NY, and SUNY New Paltz in New Paltz, NY.

"In many ways, there's nothing more powerful than writing. We sit at our desk with only a computer, or a notebook, or a pencil and paper. And we can make people fall in love. We can arrange marriages. We can start a war. We can travel back in time. We can destroy the planet and invent a new world, or we can imagine how this world will look centuries from now. When we write, we're so powerful that it's often hard to readjust and recalibrate when we leave our desks. Our characters say what we want them to say, but real people don't. Real people tell us to do things. But when we write, we are the ones in charge. The power that writing gives us transfers over—and makes us more powerful."

--FRANCINE PROSE--

Dear You

BY JULIA MERCADO, 2015

Dear You,

You are the one who never washed your hair, wore the same sweater every day, and smiled wide with blue braces. You are the one that bad days are based on. I feel we need to talk, and now's the chance.

I know you. I know every detail about you, from your crazy obsessions to your favorite shade of blue. From Julia to Julia, from silent to outspoken.

I never wanted to write to you. I never knew how, because it's near impossible to talk to the ghosts that haunt you at night. The ghosts that make me get up out of sleep and write are the ones that affect me the most.

This letter makes me feel like I'm back at my therapist's office and she's having me analyze my life. She asked me to draw my family once.

The mother, the father, and you were drawn. Having no artistic abilities, I was ashamed to show my work to my therapist. I smiled a small smile and she frowned. Immediately, there was something wrong.

"What happened to the ears?" she asked. "Does no one listen to you?" Not one person on the paper had ears. I had often told her I had issues trying to get people to listen to me. I didn't think it would affect my drawing. I never think about ears when looking at people. Ears tend to be invisible if I'm not looking at them directly. As a therapist, she made me think about it more.

I didn't want to think about it more. I didn't want to have to think about times where I was you. That blue sweater is long gone from my closet but not far off in my memory. It reminds me of times when ears and voices were hard to see and hear.

I remember having nightmares where I couldn't speak to save my life. I could feel myself scream and no sound would come out. I always wondered what that meant to me and it dawned on me; I never speak up.

Throughout my younger years, I stayed quiet and let things play out, but I remember times before you where I didn't do that. My "friends" made fun of a classmate all the time. I stayed with them to look cool; that way they wouldn't make fun of me. It was the only way to stay safe from humiliation in that class. It wasn't fair that I did this when she was always being humiliated.

They viewed Tiffany as this monster who always had a limp and a school aide with her. It was horrible. Their faces turned red with laughter every time she would walk to throw out her trash with her aide. They pretended to be her and stare into the air with blank faces.

"I think there's something wrong with her brain. She's always staring into space," they would say.

One day, they were laughing so much that spit from their mouths landed all over me; I had to get up to move. I feel like that was the best thing I had ever done in my life. "I don't want to be over there," were the words that sparked a major turning point in your life. I still remember the look of confusion on her face when I said that. Neither of us knew what effect this moment would have on us. According to you, the only thing I'm good at is being awkward. Tiffany always sees the opposite in me. She believes in me. Even when I was you, she was there for me. She saw the beauty past the insecurity and the mute voice. Tiffany knew I was better than you, the one cocooned in awkwardness. I had lost my spunk for a while, but somehow Tiffany knew it would come back. She remembered the girl who did her own thing instead of letting people walk all over her. You are the part of me that is afraid to speak up. You let people say what they wanted to say about you. You believed their rash thoughts about you. I do not want to be you anymore. I still do not speak up, and then I realize my day could have been better if I told at least one person how I truly felt. Believing in yourself is hard because everyone around you is judgmental. Who cares? Only you should care about what YOU do and what YOU say. People want to hear you, so speak loud and clear.

Whenever that past girl haunts you in your dreams, I want you to crack open this letter and read it again: out loud, in your head, or in song, until you absolutely get tired of what is in here and the message has finally gotten through. I would wish you luck in believing yourself, but that's already beginning. You're making yourself be heard in this moment, Little Miss. Keep going.

Yours truly,

You (with a voice)

JULIA MERCADO was born in Brooklyn, NY. She attended Manhattan Village Academy in New York, NY, and Dickinson College in Carlisle, PA.

Abuelo's Porch

BY MARCELA GRILLO, 2012

Coqui, coqui. Close my eyes and listen closely. I can hear. The singsong voice of the Coqui frog lulls me to sleep. In the morning, I sip *café con leche.* The black-and-white tiles of Abuelo's porch are warm under my feet. Tall coconut trees stretch into the sky over the horizon. The air smells of fresh leaves and of animals who run. Of breadfruit and mangoes and *platanos.* Abuelo's calloused hands reach up and he plucks a coconut down from the tree. Sticks a straw inside, and without a word, hands it to me. I know to take the coconut and sip directly from it. The sweet taste floods over my tongue.

Even when there is no more juice left to sip, I can still feel the tang of the coconut on the bottom of my teeth. Abuelo and I sit next to each other, my legs swinging, and every so often a film of dust sprinkles onto the bottom of my toes.

I see cars drive by. The passengers wave their hands out the car windows, yelling *hello* or an exaggerated shout of sorts that I cannot understand.

"Abuelo," I ask, turning my head to the right. I admire everything from his white cotton sleeve shirt to the way he crosses his knees. I try to mimic him but fail. "Who are all those people driving by?"

Abuelo's thin lips curve into something like a smile as he wipes a bit of coconut juice from his upper lip. "Sometimes I wish I didn't know them," he says. "But they are my friends."

I simply nod and wonder how Abuelo has so many friends when the tinted glass hides their faces.

We pass the rest of the evening watching the sun descend into the mountain's embrace. I sit on Abuelo's porch, and I know I cannot be touched.

When night falls and the roads turn into unknown paths, I pad into my room and run under the scratchy blanket. The thunder claps like an angry command, once, twice, three times.

As if he knows, Abuelo comes into the room and sits beside me. He smiles down gently and whispers that I shouldn't be scared. His hands pat my forehead before he leaves again, closing the door behind him with a soft thump, although it seems louder with all the lights out.

That's when I think I hear the front door slam. *Who is there?* I try to look for the time and then remember I don't have my own watch. I love Abuelo's watch, though. I hope he'll let me have it one day. My toes tingle underneath the blankets, and before thinking twice I escape, my toes twitching against the now-cold floor.

The door handle is grey and dented, but my hand fits around it perfectly. I open the door only slightly and hope not to get caught. I see the outline of Abuelo's thin gray hair as he stands firmly on two feet. He is blocking another man's path. I try to get a better look and stand on my tippy toes. The strange man wears a red bandana and a shirt with sleeves that are cut. His eyes are a beady dark brown. He only has two fingers. It is Samuel—Abuelo used to always invite him over for drinks.

"Go," I hear him tell the man. I can see the glint of a machete hiding behind Abuelo's back. It is the same machete he always tells me to leave hidden underneath his cracked flowerpot. The one that sits on Abuelo's porch, waiting.

MARCELA GRILLO was born in Brooklyn, New York. She attended Institute for Collaborative Education in New York, NY, and Connecticut College in New London, CT.

Three Moments in a High School Life

BY EMMA FISKE-DOBELL, 2010

Lone

Peer at yourself in the scratched smudge of a bathroom mirror. Look into those eyes, scrutinize that skin. Contemplate: Are you pretty or not? Girls have watched themselves blow smoke at the glass, applied their lipstick, even wept, facing that reflection. Your hands grip the sides of the sink. The wastebasket overflowing with brown paper towels, the cold air rattling through the sorry excuse for a window, the pigeons cooing on the ledge wrenching, tender in their familiarity. Almost a comfort.

Dreaming

You're the first one to rehearsal. You climb up the stairs to the stage, dusty and blank. Those lights that, for a brief a time as you stand beneath them, tell you who you are in the world. Wait for the other kids, who show up only so they can punch their friends with an inside joke, only so they can laugh loudly and often. You feel half asleep, walking through your day, your mind somewhere else. You sit on the edge of the stage, hands in your lap. You have a long time to wait.

Spring

Walk out through those doors on the first day of March. A season starting, high school ending. Time to slam your physics book shut forever, to run your hand over the cotton of a sundress, to forget about whether or not you should get drunk over the weekend or tell an old friend you're sorry or a new friend your secrets. Time to let scraps of unrequited love fly, like something released from a car window, above the trees, only to end up on the ground. Time to breathe into your future like air filling up a lung, to tell your family that they're not so bad, to tell the boy who sits alone that it will be okay eventually. You walk out those double doors, the weight dropping behind you. The new spring air lifting your feet off the sidewalk.

EMMA FISKE-DOBELL grew up in Brooklyn, NY. She attended NYC Lab School for Collaborative Studies in New York, NY, and McGill University in Montreal, Canada.

The Places We Came From

BY TASHI SANGMO, 2009

In the place I am from the land is evergreen and wide-open and decorated with colorful flowers in summers. The snowy mountains reach high up to the clear blue sky. The memory of cool icy breezes in the early morning on my face never dies. I was born into a nomadic family like most people in my village, living on the mountains with domestic animals like yaks and sheep, and migrating to find places where there was enough water and grass for the animals.

...

In our village, houses were made of stones and timbers, with dry logs piled up around the house to make a fence. When smoke was coming from the chimney, I could tell that the house was not empty. Dusty narrow streets stretched out from each house, and people and animals walked by every day, kicking up dirt.

...

I was born when the land of Tibet had been snatched by Communist China, in 1959, and the Dalai Lama and half of the Tibetans were forced to escape to India as refugees.

Thousands of monasteries, nunneries, and education centers were destroyed, and millions of Tibetans lost their lives asking for more rights and freedom. Families left behind in Tibet were afraid to have any discussions on political issues. I was kept from understanding the politics and history of Tibet until I escaped over the mountains to India when I was eight years old.

...

Life in the 1990s was pure and narrow: day and night, I knew only the world around me. I had no fears about what would happen in the future, since I was 100 percent sure that what I saw around me was everything there was in the world. I woke up every day with the same illiterate schedule before the red sun rose behind the mountains.

I wandered all day on the mountains along with the animals, waiting for the shadow of the trees to reach over the river so that I could go back home and play hide-and-seek with neighborhood friends. We kids liked rolling in the mud and clay until our clothes got wet and stuck to our bodies, despite the fact that we knew we'd be scolded by our parents that night.

Life in the 2000s became days filled with light because I got to India and started school.

When I was a shepherd on the mountains, the days were long, but days turned into minutes with the busy schedule of my boarding school life in India. I went to classes from 7:30 AM to 4:30 PM, and after school I had activities such as basketball, volleyball, and knitting clubs.

...

To keep from freezing, I wore hairy boots made from yak's skin and long skirts made out of sheep's skin. I also wore long-sleeved shirts and Chupa—a

Tibetan dress with a long skirt—handmade by my mom and grandma. On special occasions I wore sneakers. In India, I wore regular dress, like t-shirts and pants and sneakers bought from the local Indian stores.

...

My favorite memories of my life in Tibet are hearing the beautiful songs of the morning birds in the oak trees and feeling the warm, cozy hands of my grandma on my face, making me smile.

TASHI SANGMO was born in Tibet and grew up in India and Brooklyn, NY. She attended International High School in Brooklyn, NY, and Mount Holyoke College in South Hadley, MA.

Opening Up

BY MEEK THOMAS, 2016

Ms. Sears, our school's guidance counselor, greets me with a smile—protocol, I'm guessing, because no one is ever that happy, especially not someone whose job is to help a bunch of kids going through rough times. She reaches out to grab my shaky hand. I don't know why I am nervous. I scheduled the appointment. It's probably because I'm scared my mom might find out and think I'm seriously depressed. I'm not.

My hands clam up and twitch vigorously the closer we get to Ms. Sears's office door. She finally lets go to open it and steps aside, the jolt of her head silently letting me know it's time to come in. I cross the threshold but remain in the doorway. The red walls are the first thing I see, covered in inspirational quotes. One in bold font says: "Don't become the person that hurt you." No one hurt me—that's the first thing that comes to mind.

"You can sit anywhere you want," Ms. Sears says. I pick the farthest beanbag chair from her desk and plop down on it.

"Nya, right?" she asks. Of course she calls out the wrong name. I sigh at her mistake, already regretting my decision to speak to her.

"No," I say, and my voice cracks a bit. "My name's Meek."

"Ahh, yes. I'm sorry, hon." Ms. Sears scribbles something down on her clipboard and I repeatedly crack my knuckles, a nervous habit I've picked up over the years. "So, what did you want to speak to me about?"

I'm terrified, I don't know where I'm going. I'm lost, and I'm hoping you will just give me the answers to all my problems. "Oh, um . . ." I clear my throat. "I guess I was feeling a bit overwhelmed," I say flatly. I'm careful not to show emotion.

"Hmm." She nods. "How so?" She picks up the clipboard and pen again, awaiting my answer.

No one cares what I'm feeling. I've been living to try to please others my entire life and now I seem to have completely lost touch with myself. I want to go away for a bit. "School," I blurt out. "It's hard."

Ms. Sears looks up at me with a raised eyebrow, silently condemning my reluctance to open up, then sighs and walks my way, green Post-it and pen in hand. She plops down on the beanbag chair next to mine and sits there quietly. *Really, lady?* Time goes by and neither of us has made a sound besides my occasional sniffle, and I begin to wonder if I'm wasting my time by coming here. Then I find the courage to look her way. She has four Post-its placed in a line on the white board next to us.

"I heard you like to write," she says. My heart leaps in my throat and I nod. "So, write what you're feeling."

For the next thirty minutes, I write how I am feeling toward family, school, relationships, and inside.

My mom only cares about my grades. "How'd you do in school today?" is different from "How was your day?" She doesn't pay attention unless I'm failing.

I just want to graduate, but I don't know what comes next. I mean, I know I'm supposed to go to college, but what if that's not for me? Can I study what makes me happy or what makes money? I think of dropping out every day.

My boyfriend loves me. He's told me multiple times. I love him too, I think. He really does care about me and has pushed me the most to get some help. He's special, but I feel like I'm waiting for him to screw up, like all the others do.

Ahh, internal stuff. I know nothing about myself except for my name. I think I'm going through that "finding yourself" stage. I Googled symptoms of depression again last week just to be sure things haven't gotten worse. I think I'm good. Is it normal to be strangers with yourself?

I drop the pen in the beanbag chair. I don't realize I'm crying until Ms. Sears hands me a box of tissues. "Thanks," I sniffle.

"We've all been in this place, honey," she begins. "And sometimes it takes crawling through a whole bunch of mess, but we eventually get through it. This is part of growing up; we realize that the things around us aren't always as they seem, and right now you're just swaying in the middle of child and adult. You're a promising girl, and I know you're going to be something real special. You just gotta pick yourself up."

She steps closer to hug me and I open my arms to embrace her. When she pulls back I begin to chuckle through my tears.

"What's funny?" she asks. *That was the best Disney advice I've ever received.*

"Thanks for today," I say. "Save some more Post-its for next time."

MEEK THOMAS was born in Brooklyn, NY. She attended Uncommon Charter High School in Brooklyn, NY, and Bay Path University in Longmeadow, MA.

The First 1,578 Days in New York City

BY XIAO SHAN LIU, 2013

Right from the minute we got on the plane in China, my mother and sister depended entirely on the poor English I had learned in school. This had never happened to me; I had never used English in China, and I had never been around people using English.

After landing and the long process of immigration, I officially became a resident of New York City. My father came and picked us up outside the airport, telling us we would live with my aunt's family. Before I arrived, it was hard to think that an apartment could fit almost ten people, but we managed to make it work.

The first American culture that I experienced was Thanksgiving Day right after I arrived. It is similar to the Chinese New Year: family will come together and eat. But the food was different from what I had tried before. In my first American dinner, I ate turkey with some of the nuts stuck in its stomach and the sauce. The skin was crispy and tasted awesome with the spices, but the meat tasted unflavored and made me think that the turkey hadn't exercised for a long time, compared with the chickens we raised in China. It was a very interesting dinner for me.

I went to school right after Thanksgiving. MS 131 was a bilingual school where everyone spoke Chinese and English. The students came from different places, such as Fuzhou, Guangzhou, and Malaysia. We were what people called ESL students, or "English as a Second Language" students.

Outside of school, since I was the one with the most education in the family, I felt like I had the responsibility to help my mom and sister adjust to New York and learn to communicate. For that, I had to learn more, know more. The schoolwork wasn't enough for me, so I practiced at crowded restaurants like McDonald's and Burger King a lot, trying to use English to order food and listen to people next to me.

I also went around and watched the New York lifestyle: seeing New Yorkers walking, talking, and yelling in the street with all kinds of languages. Seeing different cars pass by, rock music was so loud blowing through the windows to the street that sometimes it spurred the passerby to dance and sing with the music.

After I arrived, New York showed me that my old view of the world was like that of the frog in the well knowing nothing of the great ocean. It was the first time I realized that the world is so big, and I was just a country girl from a small town in China. Knowing this, I became more active in my life. I joined the school activities and outside programs, I became more social and more determined with the things going on around me.

This is New York, a place that bubbles with enthusiasm and freedom. It is a city with plenty of opportunities; here I have become a more gung-ho and proactive person than I used to be. I am no longer a country girl who couldn't understand what others were talking about. I want people to know: that little Chinese girl who spent her childhood in a small town has grown up. In New York, she has become a young woman who is taking responsibility for her life and starting to fight for her dreams and goals.

XIAO SHAN LIU was born in China. She attended International High School at Union Square and City College of New York in New York, NY.

Keeping Faith

BY ZAHRAA LOPEZ, 2016

My mother was always a warrior. She was born battling the tough streets of Bed-Stuy, strong and ready to conquer the world. Quick to have her guard up and seldom trusted people. She never believed in her self-worth and she had no idea that she'd be a savior someday.

When she had us she decided she no longer wanted to linger on her past. She wanted to build a future that her babies would be proud of, an empire that would grow with us. But she didn't think she'd be able to do it on her own. The man she thought she loved grew distant, and her empire was falling. But she never lost hope. Her faith was as strong as her grip on God, refusing to let go. Two years ago, she decided to go back and get something that could never be taken away from her: an education. She struggled through many sleepless nights, and I was always beside her, doing 2 AM grammar checks without my own homework done. But seeing her walk across the stage to get her diploma made everything worth it. That piece of paper was the key to freedom—Momma, you earned it. Tears fell down my face and I was so proud, like I was the parent and she was the child.

A year later the tables turned. Now I was staying up late to edit my college applications, and through it all my mother was my biggest motivation. Soon I'll be walking across the stage to get my diploma. I am afraid of the future. But I know my mother's perseverance will continue to inspire me. When I feel like giving up I will think of her: a single mother with the weight of the world on her shoulders. When I have children one day, I hope I can be half the woman she is. Half as strong, half as kind, half as determined.

If she can do it, so can I.

ZAHRAA LOPEZ was born in the Bronx, NY. She attended Cristo Rey New York High School in New York, NY, and Howard University in Washington, D.C.

Black

BY RACHEL AGHANWA, 2015

"Black is just a color," I've heard people say. Technically, they're wrong. Black is the presence of ALL colors. But black is deeper than "just a color." Black is my roots, the vines of my family tree twisting their way across the Atlantic Ocean on a straight path to the motherland. Black is my complexion, the skin tone stretching over the canvas of my body, encasing every crevice on the surface. Black is beautiful, and black is what makes me, me.

But as a child, black was a curse.

Black meant I wasn't as pretty as the other girls in my class. Black meant chemically damaging my hair since the age of five just to get that pin-straight perfection of the girls with an ivory complexion. Black was the crayon I never used in my sixty-four-pack crayon box because my friends always said to me how dark and ugly it was.

And, to my current disappointment, I thought black meant failure.

Black was also the color of the television screen when you lost a video game, and in big white letters, it would say "you lose" or "game over" depending on what game I decided to play.

My whole life I felt like I wasn't important enough to speak so that people would listen to me, due to my skin tone. I felt as if my color was an obstacle I could never overcome.

I went through a period of self-hatred, beating myself up, trying to fix myself even though I was nowhere near broken. I would straighten my hair constantly, burning it to the root, just to be "pretty enough." I would cry endlessly when girls of all colors used to berate me because I wasn't light enough or I was "too African to actually be considered black."

It took me a while of self-inflicted mental torture to realize that being black was not hindering me but actually propelling me.

When I visited Nigeria with my mother and my brother, I remember our driving past a billboard that read "black is not a color, but is actually an attitude."

That was the day I realized, why should I hate myself over something I have no control over? Why should I see what I am as a curse instead of a blessing?

After I finally came to terms with myself, I looked around and realized that my story was a sad one told twice over. There are many other girls with my skin color that went and are still going through this disheartening journey I struggled through as a child.

But my mission now is to release all the black girls from the shackles society has weighed down on them, and bring them to finally see how beautiful they are.

Black is beautiful, and black is me.

RACHEL AGHANWA was born in Brooklyn, NY. She attended Queens Gateway to Health Sciences Secondary School in Queens, NY, and Temple University in Philadelphia, PA.

The Hijabi

BY NISHAT ANJUM, 2013

At eight years old, I went to a funeral. Looking back now, that funeral may have been the beginning of my prolonged evolution. That funeral was the first time I had seen a corpse; it was also the first time I saw so many people wear white. In Islam, white is the color of death. I don't remember who had died—just being stuck in a house full of weeping strangers.

I was ecstatic going home; in the car my mom put a gift from my aunt in my lap. The scarf was onyx-colored and silky in my hands. With streetlights blurring by, it seemed silver in places, and in my drowsy condition, I made out the words *Calvin Klein*. This hijab was one of many, as I later found out, but at eight I believed that it was my own special scarf.

From then on, I wore that hijab almost every week to Sunday school. Eventually I wore it to certain family dinners and parties. I noticed two things. One, it was easier to get ready without having to do my hair. And two, it was easier for me to speak to people. I wasn't my usual socially awkward self. Putting that scarf on was like putting on a mask of sorts—at least at first.

It wasn't until the summer of 2010 that I gave serious thought to wearing the hijab. For the past two years I had been going to a summer camp for teenage hijabis, Muslim women who choose to cover their hair. The best part of this camp—or not, depending on your perspective—was that it took place entirely in the city. We had BBQs, beach trips, and games, as well as lectures from prominent Islamic figures. During my second year at this camp I reached a realization.

One of the lecturers was an African American man who had converted to Islam as a teenager. They say that respect is earned, not given. If there was any better way to earn a person's respect, then he would have beaten it. If I hadn't been born into a Muslim family I don't believe I would've converted to Islam until I was older. To make such a life-changing decision at such a young age is staggering to contemplate. I listened to this man's tale of how he was abused and ridiculed for becoming a Muslim and saw how easy my own life had been. In that moment, I decided to take the jump and wear the hijab. When I walked up to my friends on that first day of high school, none of them batted an eyelash or looked taken aback at my new wardrobe choice, as I had feared. They simply said hello and demanded to know why I hadn't been in contact with any of them.

My background is filled with colors, sounds, loud jewelry, and music. I grew up watching my aunts and cousins wearing colorfully magical hijabs; some that sparkle and some that shine. I also come from a background of strong women. Women who would never agree to be "oppressed."

In my mother's time, not many women from Bangladesh wore the hijab. My mother herself chose to wear the hijab eight years ago, after she had recovered somewhat from lupus, an incurable autoimmune disease. I wouldn't say that religion is the most dominating factor in my life; it is, however, a major aspect. A lot of Middle Eastern cultures have been mixed in with Islam itself. Wherever Islam has spread, it has blended with that region's culture, making the certain "Islamic" laws or regulations that rule countries different based on the countries' influences and surrounding areas. There are in fact fifty official Islamic countries in the world and therefore probably fifty different versions of

Islam, all with the same underlying faith, prayers, and religious text—the Quran.

The hijab is meant to be a choice, worn out of the love of God and modesty. It is meant to spur your faith in God and to make you stronger when you are doubtful. It is meant to make its wearers grateful for their bodies and to cherish what God has given them. When you force a girl or woman to wear the hijab you are defeating its purposes. Instead of teaching them to love themselves and their religion, it may end up making them insecure and scornful of anything to do with Islam. I've seen this happen so many times with many of my friends whose parents force them to cover their hair.

After three years of wearing the hijab all the time, it has become a part of me. Like some people feel weird without their glasses or hair tied up, I feel weird being out in public without my hijab. My socially awkward self has also faded to a point of nothing, though I suspect it will always be there. My confidence was born out of the hijab and I just hope that other Muslim women will be able to draw strength from it as I have.

NISHAT ANJUM was born in Bangladesh. She attended Susan E. Wagner High School in Staten Island, NY, and Brooklyn College in Brooklyn, NY.

A Touch of Memory between Amsterdam and a Guy Named Columbus

BY JASMINE HOLLOWAY, 2008

We set our scene at 125 West 109th Street, between Columbus and Amsterdam—my home. I have lived here all my life, a few blocks from Nancy, but this neighborhood holds different memories for me. I remember waiting in my building's lobby on a cold winter's day for the small yellow bus to arrive and pick up my brother for school. The number "12" painted on the left side of the lobby door in brown and the number "5" painted on the right. I always wondered if "5" was ever lonely there underneath the dim, shaded light. I remember riding my new pink-and-white tricycle in the outside yard of my building, one story above ground, and the regular dirty streets of Amsterdam. In between the dark brown trees that hovered over my small body, I tried to avoid every crack and misplaced rock on the ground. Yet still, I would fall. I never rode that bike again. I remember walking down the narrow hallways of my home in 8B and the cold sensation of my two little chubby feet touching the smooth tiles on the floor. I remember moving into 11H, a new apartment much bigger than the last. Three rooms instead of two, the distance between my family and me wasn't apparent at the time, as the warmth of my new home wrapped around my body like a warm blanket. I knew this was forever. Tender years came and went. I blindly sat by thinking these four walls and everything they hold are immortal, nothing damaged, nothing lost, just kept together.

That was until materialistic dreams turned into concrete reality, crashing down on top of my head like heavy rain. Moving again, 10K gave each of us our own space, dividing my family members one by one, making the space that existed between us larger. It tugged at the strings of my adolescent heart to leave my worn-out church dresses in the vacant closets of the house that isn't my home anymore. It was the place where the rest of my estranged family broke their last bread together, before their once-intertwined paths in life crossed no more.

Now, I have removed my still-framed life and joined the fast-paced world, *outside* of the walls that cocooned me. I brush my chubby ebony fingers along the cold, rusty black bars of a vacant lot owned by Con Edison next to my building. The wind creeps up on me as I pass the old weathered signs saying, "Bush lies, who dies" or "Need a house maid?"

I stand at the corner and see the dark, gloomy cathedral, the old newspapers whirling like a tornado on the ground, leaves blowing across my feet. Home isn't far from here . . . from here, it's never too far.

JASMINE HOLLOWAY grew up in New York, NY. She attended Urban Assembly Media High School in New York, NY, and LaGuardia Community College and City College in New York, NY.

The Search

BY IDAMARIS PEREZ, 2012

Funny how an ordinary start of one's day can transform into something extraordinary. I observe through the crystal-clean window of my dad's lime-green Toyota all of these conch houses. I lay my head on the back of my car seat as I sigh, bored of seeing an endless parade of wooden shingles and gabled roofs. *Estamos aqui ya?* "Areee weee theree yeet?" I ask my parents in an impatient, childish tone. *Casi, casi.* "Almost there," they respond in unison.

When it comes to conversing with my parents, Spanish is my customary language since they both were born and raised in the Dominican Republic. *Que Viva La Republica Dominicana!* "Long Live Dominican Republic!" screams that pitched voice in my head. I'm very patriotic about my beloved Dominican Republic—the jewel of the Caribbean Sea.

I would always go to the Dominican Republic every summer without fail—until now. I'm annoyed about the fact that I have to go visit my great-grandma in Florida. I am not in the mood for it, but what can an eleven-year-old girl possibly do other than obey her authorities. Besides, my great-grandma barely visits me and my family in New York.

She doesn't care about us; why do my parents care to visit her?

Believe me, I'm not even a fanatic about architecture, but here I am admiring this house that my great-great-grandfather built with his own hands. My great-grandmother's house is not even a conch house. It's a very long, wooden barn house. For some weird reason, the presence of this house makes me tingle with excitement, like it is inviting me to discover the wonders of my ancestors' past. I rush inside this beauty and see my great-grandmother; she has aged so much from the last time she came to visit us. She appears to be a hundred years old. Her cinnamon, heart-shaped face screams *tired* with those three heavy wrinkles on her forehead, and she already has a tiny hunchback. But her gleaming, hazel eyes reveal a youthful spirit. She starts commenting in Spanish how glad she is to see me, how I morphed into this beautiful young Dominican princess, and that she missed me a lot.

Disinterested in her comments, I back off to explore the house; everything else, except her, seems interesting. I ascend a staircase that leads me into the attic, which is cluttered with antique, dusty items. I begin my search and find an album of ancestors and start gazing at these faces. Some of my ancestors were attractive, but some were not so good-looking. While I flip through the pictures, a paper slips out of one of the pages. I pick up the old, dull paper, which is a map. "It's treasure hunt time!"

I follow the directions of the map until I encounter a sturdy mahogany trunk. Fortunately, it does not have a lock so I do not have to waste my time searching for the keys. I open it and, wow, I discover a pair of tattered books about Juan Bosch, who was a Dominican scholar, political activist, and even president of Dominican Republic. "This is some fancy treasure," I quip sarcastically. "I should be in the *Guinness Book of World Records* for finding the dumbest treasure ever."

I feel the presence of somebody behind me; I turn my head impulsively and find my great-grandmother, staring sorrowfully yet nostalgically at the books. She turns her attention to me and caresses my shoulders. She begins to narrate for me her childhood story, that she and her sister were inseparable, sister soul mates. They were very attached, wore the same humble outfits too, and what they enjoyed doing the most was reading Juan Bosch's stories. Until a tragic fate befell them and left a footprint of pain in my great-grandma's heart. Her sister, in her teens, died tragically in a car accident, her head cracked wide open. My great-grandma was present for that car accident and saw her sister in that traumatic state. She says that the memory will always linger in her head. Luckily, great-grandma survived with some cuts and bruises. After her sister's death, she decided to conceal the books inside the trunk because she couldn't cope with the painful memory.

A fragment of her identity flew with her sister into heaven.

I try to stifle my tears, but the dam breaks and streams trickle down my cheeks. My great-grandma sheds a few tears too, but I know that she's mourning inside. I embrace my great-grandma tightly, which pacifies her. *Gracias mi hija*: "Thank you my darling," she says. And we both leave our ancestor's room holding our hands, together.

IDAMARIS PEREZ was born in New York, NY. She attended St. Jean Baptiste High School and Manhattan College in New York, NY.

The One I Need

BY JANIAH TAYLOR, 2017

Kareem is quiet. Rarely ever speaking, and when you ask him a question, he will give you a low grunt, meaning either yes, no, or leave me alone. Though caring, he won't show it much. Try and touch him, he'll slap you. Give him a hug? Oh no, you get a rough push to the ground. That is his way of being nice.

He never seemed to care about life before; he was living just because he seemed obligated to do so. He never seemed happy. When I was younger and I cried, which was a lot, he would always tell me to shut up. I would never go to him for support because he had what only seemed to be hate for me and he would always just push me away.

This day was different.

I was about nine years old. My brother, only a year-and-a-half older, was in charge. A few days before this, we went to see a Broadway Christmas show. Our mom got the last of a very delicate ornament as a souvenir. It was pretty large, about the size of a lightbulb. It was blue and had characters from the show on it.

That day we were putting up the tree, and Kareem and I were hanging the last of the ornaments.

"Let's put this one up," my brother said, pointing to the Broadway ornament.

"We shouldn't; Mom said not to touch it."

"We'll surprise her; it's okay." I caved in and helped him unwrap it and bring it to the tree.

We started to fight over who got to put it up and then CRACK. There it was, broken in half on the floor. At first, we tried to fix it with glue. Then my mother's footsteps came toward us.

Kareem threw the ornament in the box and I hid the materials. We bolted up the stairs, and before I could lock myself in the bathroom, my mom's voice shook the house.

There was nothing my brother and I could do. In the old, dark, eerie hallway only the light from the bathroom aimed brightly at my mother's face.

"I ask you one simple thing, a simple task, and you can't seem to do that," she started. I stood there straddling the bathroom and the hallway barely looking at her, my eyes peering to the ground. My brother stood by his bedroom door, which was basically like a closet, giving the same blank stare as usual. I tried to open my mouth but her eyes stopped me. The look in her eyes gave me a feeling that you should never feel. It seemed so cold and heartless, when it was unintended. I believed my brother felt this, too, for when she looked at him, he seemed scared for the first time.

"You should both be ashamed. When I ask something, it should never be questioned. Do you know how much that Christmas ornament cost? Where will I find one like that again?" she went off.

She looked at my brother, who stood silent in his doorway. "Nothing to say, Kareem?" she said sarcastically. He shook his head without even looking up. "What about you, Janiah?" she said, glaring at my weak body.

"I'm sorry, Mommi," I sputtered out, holding back my tears. "Sorry won't fix what you did," she said, walking away. The stairs creaked as she went down to the basement. It was only silence, and I remember Kareem's heartbroken eyes toward me. The wind rustled against the window and the house seemed abandoned. Neither of us knew what to say. Kareem came toward me, trying to grab my hand, and I went into the bathroom and closed the door, only remembering the sorrow in his face before I was alone.

I sat down on the dull-colored toilet seat and cried my eyes out. The bathroom seemed sad like me, with the off-white tiles and the broken window that let in the draft and gave an ominous light. This was my safe space. The light brown granite sink was my armrest. I got up to look at myself in the three-paneled mirror. My eyes were bloodshot and my face looked drained. I could not bear to see myself.

When I opened the door, it was just my weary shadow there to greet me. I turned, slowly, to find my brother standing there. The tension in his eyes made me nervous, so I looked down.

"I'm sorry," was all I could seem to spill out. I felt the tears creep up again, and thinking he would yell or just walk away, I felt his arms wrap around me so gentle like a blanket. He cried with me; I felt his tears fall on my shoulder. He held me tighter and he did not want to let go. And neither did I.

JANIAH TAYLOR was born in Brooklyn, NY. She attended Academy for Young Writers in Brooklyn, NY.

"I think that what our society teaches young girls—it's something that's quite difficult for even older women and self-professed feminists to shrug off—is the idea that likability is an essential part of you, of the space you occupy in the world, that you're supposed to twist yourself into shapes to make yourself likable, that you're supposed to hold back sometimes, pull back, don't quite say, don't be too pushy, because you have to be likable. I say that's bullshit. Forget about likability. If you start thinking about being likable you are not going to tell your story honestly, because you are going to be so concerned with not offending, and that's going to ruin your story. So, forget about likability. The world is such a wonderful, diverse, and multifaceted place that there's somebody who's going to like you; you don't need to twist yourself into shapes."

— CHIMAMANDA NGOZI ADICHIE —

Why Won't You Stop!?

BY KIRBY-ESTAR LAGUERRE, 2016

Unfortunately, the past eighteen years of my life have been filled with endless frustrations—specifically, things I wish people would *not* do and things I wish people would *not* say.

Here are some of the most notorious:

1) Don't ever say to me these two hackneyed lines: "These are the best years of your life," and "One day you'll laugh at this." My cousins told me that high school would be the best four years of my life. But if the best four years of my life happened before I turned eighteen years old and the average life span is seventy-nine years—one hundred and one years for me, if I'm blessed with my great grandmother's genes—what will the other sixty-one to eighty-three years of my life be like? Especially since high school wasn't all that great. Rumors. Heartache. Popularity contests. Fakers. That is supposed to be the highlight of my life? I desperately hope not. My cousins also told me that one day I would laugh at all of that. Oddly enough, I do not think I will ever find the fact that my best friend dated the guy I was in love with amusing.

2) Don't have your TV, movie, or fiction characters say "NOOOOOO!" as if dragging out the letter *O* could keep something bad from

happening. If life were truly that easy, I would be saying "NOOOOOO" all over the place. "NOOOOOO" when my AP Chemistry teacher wants to give us a test on gas laws and "NOOOOOO" when Kanye West goes on yet again another Twitter rant. But, of course, this has not yet been made possible in my time, and I am left leaving short response questions blank and reading tweets about Kanye's ego. So, news flash: saying "NOOOOOO" is in no way helping your characters' "critical"—though in my eyes overly dramatic and totally unrealistic—situation.

3) Don't portray every person who finds out that they have cancer as sad and miserable. My friend Elise did not cry, did not dramatically sob, and certainly did not ask, "How long do I have left?" like the characters you see in movies or read about in books do. Instead, when Dr. Harlow told her that she had been diagnosed with breast cancer, these were her exact words: "Will I still be able to have chicken wings for dinner?"

4) Stop making me look for a "Prince Charming" (a.k.a. the amazing man who makes it his mission to rescue the damsel in distress. According to Urban Dictionary, "he is handsome and romantic and makes all girls swoon"). I don't want one.

5) Stop telling me, "Love isn't always enough." Love should always be enough. If what I feel for someone is authentic, passionate, consuming, and simply beautiful in its rawness, it should work.

6) Stop calling me an "Oreo." I am not shaped like a circle. I do not have cream filling, and the word "Oreo" is not stamped across my torso. Speaking correctly does not equate to being white.

7) Stop asking me "Are you okay?" if all you want to hear is "I'm fine." We both know that anything more than those two words is too much for you to handle.

8) Don't text me an "I miss you" when I am finally starting to move on.

9) Don't tell me I am not allowed to feel that way.

10) Stop saying that I am "pretty for a black girl."

11) Stop comparing me to her. And her. And her.

12) Don't underestimate me.

I am begging you.

Please don't.

Please stop.

KIRBY-ESTAR LAGUERRE was born in Brooklyn, NY. She attended The Leon Goldstein High School for the Sciences in Brooklyn, NY, and Vanderbilt University in Nashville, TN.

The Feminist in Me

BY TUHFA BEGUM, 2014

It started with an insult, when we collided at the front door of school at eight o'clock on a Monday morning and I dropped an armful of feminist posters. They scattered across the threshold and back down the steps. He stood watching as I struggled to pick them up and tuck them under my arm.

"What's the matter with you anyways?" he asked. He had that slouchy look on his face that some boys covet.

"Excuse me?"

"Why don't you take cooking class like the other girls do? At least you'd learn something useful."

Before I could answer, the bell rang and we went our separate ways to class.

I was a feminist long before I knew what the word meant. I was born in Bangladesh, unaware that I was the first female in my family to be delivered in a hospital, the first to receive a birth certificate. Later, my grandfather defied gender norms by teaching me to read and write in English. In the mosque, he seated me up front with him and the other men, rather than placing me in a dark corner with the other women and children.

My mother never received these benefits. When she was born, my grandparents were young, poor, and living in a backward village. They arranged her marriage to my father at a young age. Our female ancestors married young, then spent most of their time relentlessly cooking, cleaning, and caring for children. Even today in Bangladesh, the expectation for a girl is to have no expectations.

I immigrated to the United States with my parents when I was three years old. While other little girls followed Disney princesses, I imagined a princess who could save herself and her kingdom. I identified with Susan Pevensie, who was cast out of mythical Narnia because she refused to conform. In middle school, we had to create a board game using historical events. I added a new category to my board called "The Suffrage Movement and Feminism." A family friend studied my board and asked, "What about men's rights? We carry the burden of your feminine nonsense."

In ways I didn't fully appreciate, my mother was my role model. While the mothers of many of my classmates were doctors or lawyers, my mother juggled working a minimum-wage job serving fast food and taking care of her family. If others disparaged me, my mother encouraged me to work hard and persevere against obstacles.

In high school, I took extra courses, volunteered at the Housing Works Bookstore, raised money for United Nations programs, and received the many benefits of belonging to Girls Write Now. Last summer, I interned at the Bella Abzug Leadership Institute, founded by the daughter of "Battling Bella" herself. Here, feminism came alive as we declared that women's rights *are* human rights.

At that point, my beliefs turned into activism. I began making posters about the global subjugation and abuse of women and taping them up at school. I staged little events in the hallways and handed out flyers. Mostly, my efforts were ignored.

My mother always stood by me, from the warm glasses of milk she would hand to me during late-night study sessions, to the Girls Write Now annual public readings, where she clapped the loudest when I read my work. Even so, her long work hours and my demanding academic schedule meant that we spent little time together.

One afternoon, after having two wisdom teeth removed, I sulked around the house until, finally, I followed my mother into uncharted territory—the kitchen. I never helped out in the kitchen. My mother understood that I feared stepping inside even once would lead to never stepping out.

As I stood in the doorway, watching her—she was wearing her faded blue jeans and *salwar kameez* while she prepared dinner—I saw that she looked happy. She was gossiping on the phone with a friend and chopping onions at the same time. (I don't know *how* she does this.) I had never wondered if my mother was happy or not. I took for granted that she was always there, providing everything we needed.

My mother said "goodbye" to her friend, hung up the phone, and continued working. Her black hair caught the light, and streaks of gray glimmered as she pushed her hair off her face. She hummed along to the Beatles on the radio, and I remembered what my writing mentor once told me: "Even in spaces of confinement, women can find liberation."

I lingered in the doorway until she noticed me. "It's just dal," she said, stirring lentils that were soaking in a pot of water. "Come, clean the next bag. Pick out the tiny stones." First step. Second step. On the third step, I found myself inside the kitchen, standing close to my mother. I opened the other bag of lentils. We sang "Lucy in the Sky with Diamonds" as we worked. The next time someone tells me to abandon my posters and take cooking class, I'll say, "I already know how to cook. My mother taught me!"

TUHFA BEGUM was born in Sylhet, Bangladesh. She attended Vanguard High School in New York, NY, and New York University in New York, NY.

Saturday Morning

BY MITZI SANCHEZ, 2011

"Mitzi, wake up."

"Come on, Ma, let me sleep." I'm already annoyed. My cozy bed doesn't want to let me go. But wait a minute, the buttery, salty, and savory smell of bacon, egg, and cheese travels across my room and I just can't wait to taste it. I feel the food already in my mouth.

"Mitzi, go to the laundromat, and buy me a phone card." She made me eat so fast I'm stuffed. Still that breakfast was banging. Suddenly, I hear the grumpy old Colombian lady yelling at the garbage man for no reason. She thinks I stalk her. Seriously. She gets me so frustrated. The Clorox is nowhere to be found. Doing the laundry pisses me off because I have to wash my sister's and my mom's clothes *and* mine. "Don't forget about the phone card," Mama screams, as if I'm deaf. The elevator is not working again. This blue cart is too heavy; I have to bump it down the stairs. I try to be calm, but the cart is almost the same height as me. I feel like I'm dragging my sister. As I pull the door, I see the super with his marine-blue shirt and those circular glasses he's always wearing. He's sweeping up. With his husky voice, he greets in Spanish.

"Buenos días." I smile and keep pulling the cart out the door. I see those bald Chinese men again. I turn around and the old Chinese ladies are coming outside, holding big cans of rice and meat, and wearing those hideous polka-dot pajamas. I wonder if they are lining up to get food. They must be homeless or maybe they are relatives. Look at how they smile at each other. Wow, that's amazing. I wonder to myself if they do that in China. That's generous of them. No one else gives out food in Jackson Heights.

It's windy today. I am trying to roll this cart and it gets stuck. How I hate this bumpy street. I have four more blocks to walk. I wonder if this cart's going to get stuck again. I hope not—it's embarrassing. Everybody's going to stare at me and make fun of me.

I hope there are no people at the laundromat, especially those nosy and loud Indian women. They're always there gossiping about everything. Surprise, four of them are here wearing those fancy, glittering dresses. They won't stop talking. Nice, now I have to listen to them. Why are they laughing and looking at me? They must be talking about me. I shake my head and try to ignore them, which is easy since they speak another language I don't even understand. Still, they give me a headache.

Great, my mom didn't give me any money for the laundry. I have to use mine. These quarter machines better be working.

This is taking forever. Finally, forty-five minutes later I fold my clothes and my sister's, and my mom's. Why did my sister stay home? She should be here helping me with the laundry. Damn, she's so lazy.

I grab the cart and head back home. WAIT! My mom's phone card. There are two grocery stores; on the left and the right. Which one should I go to? Umm, on the right corner, the owner is from Poland. He's a really nice man. He always smiles at me when I go, but he barely understands me. On the left, the owner is Dominican. Every time I go there, he gives me this mean, dirty look, and it makes me feel uncomfortable. But he understands my language. I'll go with the nice Polish man.

My mom never told me what phone card she wanted. Which one should I get? There are so many. Should I get her the $2, the $5, or the $10 one? It's my money; I'll buy her the $2 one.

I'm thirsty, and I need something to wake me up. I should buy me something. Perhaps a little treat, a Monster drink; I love those drinks.

I'm done with the laundry. You know what? I'm going to sit on that old concrete bench and enjoy my drink.

Look who's there. My sister came to help me pull the cart. She brought me an orange juice. Maybe she's not so bad after all.

MITZI SANCHEZ was born in Mexico. She attended Flushing International High School in Queens, NY, and Lehman College in Bronx, NY.

A Walk through Racism

BY BIANCA JEFFREY, 2017

I truly didn't see that coming. I didn't think our regular walk in the park would have ended so horribly. Cam, my friend of six years, caught me by surprise. In that moment, I thought I could talk to her on a complex level, but I guess I was wrong. Our conversation on racism ended in confusion for me and frustration for her. What concerned me was that we'd been friends for a long time and only joked about the stupidity of racism, but the one time we spoke on a serious note there was a disagreement.

Earlier that day at chorus rehearsal we were having a group discussion and the topic of racism in the media came up. Cam decided to join the conversation and said something I found questionable: *"All white people are racist."*

"Cam, do you really think all white people are racist?" I asked.

Cam responded harshly and defensively, "Yes."

I looked at her, confused. She seemed upset. I was surprised by her reaction. I looked around for the person she was showing this anger toward and soon came to the conclusion that it was me. I wondered if I had asked her in a rude way or even had harsh intention in my voice. I internally questioned the way I approached her. She said something about "having the right to her opinion." I agreed but was still confused about the answer she was giving me as she continued raising her voice. I told myself to stay controlled and think from her perspective.

I knew for sure that Cam had encountered some racism in her life. I had to take that into account when I thought about how she sees herself as a young black woman in society. I had to think about the obstacles she goes through at school and in her day-to-day life. I thought about how I had never experienced racism like her, but I did experience enough to understand what racism is and how it feels. Although we had slightly different experiences as young black girls, I was still able to see the picture beyond my own. My fear was that she wouldn't be able to do the same.

I *do not* believe all white people are racist. If I were Cam, my words would have been slightly different. I would've used the word *some* when describing a specific group of people. I understand how important it is to voice your beliefs and I don't believe in blaming a group of people for the downfalls of some within them. I feel when people say the word *all* when describing a group of people, categorizing them as one is very ignorant and unfair.

My beliefs made it hard for me to know where I stood in my friendship with Cam. I had to ask myself if I wanted to continue a friendship with a person of her mind-set—always closed off. Realizing Cam wouldn't change her opinion, I was worried she would always think from that perspective. I didn't think she was a bad person and I always enjoyed hanging out with her. Cam's personality was the main reason we became friends. It seemed like we agreed on everything. After our argument, I realized that we won't always think the same way and we don't have to. Although it was really tough for me, I learned I have to stick up for what I believe in even if that means losing those close to me.

BIANCA JEFFREY was born in New York, NY. She attended High School of Fashion Industries in New York, NY.

Space

BY TAMMY CHAN, 2011

Kid

"When are you going to throw away all those science boards? They're taking up space!" my mom would ask me every time she took out the garbage. I never could quite answer her because a part of me didn't ever want to let them go. It was a collection of four boards, each decorated with construction paper and glitter. They were three years' worth of my brilliantly and geniusly put together science projects.

Third grade: *Float or Sink.* "Oh, this pencil case is definitely gonna sink!" I said. "Yeah right, I bet it floats!" my partner, Kayla said. It sank. I was pretty genius, I'd say.

Fourth grade: *Which Bean Grows the Fastest.* The lima bean, of course! I was right. Like I said, genius.

Fifth grade: *Do Plants Grow More in the Dark or the Light.* Light, of course! Need I say?

Genius.

I was proud of my projects, always boasting about them when I'd have to carry the large tri-board to school the morning of the science fair. It was HUGE, much bigger than my small stature could handle while walking the three long blocks to school. My mom walked beside me, holding my book bag so that I could be a big girl for those few minutes, lugging the board to school all by myself. By the time I'd get to school, there'd be creases near the bottom two corners from the poster dragging along the ground as I walked. But what really mattered—the colors, the glitter, the fact that my guess had been proven—was intact. Bringing them home was just as bad, but what choice did I have? I couldn't just let the teacher throw them away—not after all that effort.

Now

I should have thrown the science boards away at the school, like all the other kids. I'd watch them after the science fair, laughing as they demolished their projects by kicking them, throwing them, and sliding on them across the gymnasium floor. But not me. Three years I did it. Three years in a row I stayed up late decorating the board, adding those last touches of glitter and drawing the final squiggly lines.

Third grade: The classic float-or-sink experiment (or, to sound fancy, "measuring an object's buoyancy"), in which we threw random objects into the tub filled with water and ended up having a mini-water fight in the bathroom.

Fourth grade: Which bean grows the fastest, employing the bootleg method of growing them in a Ziploc bag with a square of paper towel and staples to support the beans' roots?

Fifth grade: Do plants grow more in the dark or light? Are you kidding me?

The three classics of science fair experiments, the ones every kid in the school did. Did they measure my intelligence? Not at all.

I would kill to have projects like those again for school. In high school, there's no more need for crayons, colored pencils, markers, construction paper—and especially not glitter. I miss those days when the hardest assignment you had was a science fair project. Now it's just papers—black print on a white background. BORING! I used to have time, time to kill—staying up until, at the latest, NINE O'CLOCK! I even daringly stayed up to 9:30 PM once, JUST once because I ran out of glue and had to rummage all over the house to find something sticky.

Nothing could have stopped me before, but now—everything could. Time. Work. School. College. Parents. Boyfriend. Friends. Hunger. Coldness. Hotness. Crazy weather. Snow after seventy-degree warmth. Nothing to watch on TV. Tiredness. iPhone dying. Forgot my headphones. Annoying buskers on the train—the untalented ones. Wrong-number calls. Wrong-number calls at 4:30 in the morning. No gum in my bag. Broken nail. Bad hair days. Hair not cooperating. No more money on MetroCard. Spending a big chunk of my paycheck on a new MetroCard. Unnecessary random bag frisks in the train station during the morning rush hour AND afternoon rush hour. Fat policemen in their cars blocking the bus stop. No buses in the morning. The twenty-minute walk to the train. Crowded trains. Morning commutes. Tourists. Crappy coffee. Drama. Drama. Drama. Drama queens. Drama kings. Just drama.

Some days it's hard to tell if I'll sink or float.

TAMMY CHAN grew up in Forest Hills, Queens. She attended Talent Unlimited High School in New York, NY, and Syracuse University in Syracuse, NY.

Who Am I?

BY BRITTNEY NANTON, 2015

If I could express myself in three words, I don't think I would be able to. You see, I don't quite know how to describe myself. Also, I don't feel like it would be right to just label myself in only three words. But if I had to, I think I would choose the words *different*, *introverted*, and *kind*. Though I am many more words than just these three, I think these are the words you would use if you're meeting me for the first time. If so, you are right, but I have more to me than just that. I also like going on the internet and staying home. Part of that is because I have no one to hang out with, and the other part is because I like to be by myself sometimes. Some people think that's a wrong thing, though, to be alone. I don't think so. Being alone isn't a bad thing, but, when you actually feel alone, then that's something.

I have a lot of fears. I think I'm mostly scared of everything, or maybe it's just my anxiety that makes me fearful. I don't like bugs, doctor visits, closed-in spaces, the dark, being in groups, and mostly everything else you can think of. I sometimes feel as though having those fears limits me on the certain things that teens my age are doing. While other kids are partying and making memories that they'll keep forever, I'm home alone blogging about random things. People always tell me that I should be more like an actual teen, but mostly I disagree with them. I don't want to be partying until 7 AM and forgetting what happened the night before. I want to do what makes me happy. The terrible thing about my anxiety is that sometimes I'm uncomfortable in situations.

I am scared. As I have matured from a stubborn little girl into a teen, I've learned about my surroundings. I've lost the young, naive look in my eyes and have replaced it with a sense of anger and anxiousness. So much has changed. So many things have now become a part of my life, it's like I'm finally starting to live. I'm finally starting to observe my surroundings and learn about the world and how harsh it can be. The people that I once thought were the good guys are actually the ones that are against me. Being a black teenager in a city where so many of us are viewed as nothing more than garbage is tough. I've even started to worry for my black and brown male friends, for they have been targeted as the enemy since the second they left their mother's womb. They speak differently, dress in clothes that make them look "dangerous" and harmful to others. They, themselves, have learned to fear pale-skinned men with a blue uniform and badge, because they are the ones that have taken away their fellow brothers. In school, instead of learning about algebra and historical literature, I'm learning about ways to make myself seem invisible in front of the police. "Be polite," they tell me, "whatever you do, keep your hands where the police can see them." I've thought about how other teenagers in the world don't have to worry about dying while on their way to the store or getting arrested simply for being a darker skin tone. They don't have a target on their back while melanin boys and girls are born with it stamped on them as if it's some kind of birthmark. The little girl that once viewed the police as my heroes is gone. I now fear that they can take my life without any hesitation. As a young teenage black girl, I am scared. I am so much more than a stereotype. So much more than what you'd expect a girl like me to be. I am stronger than people make me out to be; I have so many goals that I have yet to achieve. I want to knock down the stereotype that has been pinned down on me. I am so much more than the "typical black girl." I am beautiful, I am fearless, and I am strong enough to not let the hatred toward people like me sink me down to the pits where they believe that I belong.

I am a human. I am a target. I am not afraid.

BRITTNEY NANTON was born in New York, NY. She attended Landmark High School in New York, NY, and Brandeis University in Waltham, MA.

Stunned Silence

BY WINKIE MA, 2015

I had been walking for thirty minutes, yet I still couldn't figure out if I was cold from the March breeze biting at my cheeks that Sunday morning or from the chill tickling my spine. I kept my head down, staring at the splatters of blackened gum on the pavement. I had to step carefully around shattered Heineken bottles, and I was only an inch away from stomping on a fresh glob of spit.

Silence.

I glanced up, seeing colossal brick buildings, all red and identical. I decided I could go to one of the convenience shops around me until I felt safe to walk again. To my dismay, all their windows were plastered with FOR RENT signs. Bright purple-and-orange graffiti littered their metal shutters. I tightened my jaw, unable to shake off the eerie sensation.

You're almost at Janet's house, I reminded myself, *if there are even houses there . . .*

All the neighborhoods I had known had smiling people and colorfully-chalked sidewalks, but never had I been in such a desolate place. I hoped that it was Fifty-Seventh Street already, where she lived. Soon I would be there, and soon we would be finished with the art project, and soon I would be out of this neighborhood for good. But it was only Sixty-Third Street, and I silently reprimanded myself for not taking another route.

My panic worsened when I caught sight of four men one long block ahead. They stood in front of a giant shutter. Though their voices were muffled, I could make out cusses directed at the few people who passed by, and even at such a distance, the smoke from their cigarettes was repulsive. Fright pervaded my senses. My eyes widened. Anxiously, I looked to see if I could go elsewhere, but the opposite sidewalk was closed off.

This was the only place to walk through.

Maybe Janet can come pick me up.

Keep cool.

They're gonna kill me.

They're harmless!

As I approached, I strayed right by the curb in hopes of going unnoticed. My mother had always warned me to stay away from these types of men, but I reassured myself that they had the morality not to bother me. I loosened up even more after realizing that all the people they'd harassed were adults. *I'm fourteen*, I thought. *I'm a minor. They won't do anything.*

But when I looked up, the man on the right already had his gaze set on me.

He took a puff from his cigarette and smirked, eyes trailing from the top of my beanie to the bottom of my boots. "Hey, you goin' anywhere?"

The man next to him followed suit. "Yeah, Mami, need a little help?" he hollered in a raspy voice.

My pace quickened. As I walked briskly past them, I tried to block their raucous laughter out. I hid my face deeper into my scarf in an attempt to become invisible, though it was no use. I already felt completely exposed. The men could see right through me, could smell the dripping fear. I was so uneasy that their continuous taunts became white noise in my ears.

My heart had a thundering pound. I turned around at the next block, relieved to see that they hadn't followed me. They were just blurred figures in the background, smoking and waiting for another person to shout at. After a while, they were out of sight.

I teetered down the pavement. Any thought of the art project had vanished. Instead, my mind was flooded with the sound of their heavy voices. I shivered when I thought of their ravenous eyes scanning my body, and pulled my jacket closer to my chest. I glanced behind me again and again, and once more for good measure to make sure they weren't following me.

All of a sudden, the fear became fury. My fingernails dug deeper into my palms with every angry thought. I was disgusted at what they did. I was furious that I gave off such a vulnerable impression. Would anything have changed if I stood up for myself instead? Would I feel better now?

In my head, I created a different scenario. I pictured myself with my chin tilted upward and my shoulder blades pressed against each other. I pictured myself standing as tall as a five-foot girl could go. I pictured myself telling each and every one of them: "Go to hell!"

But all that had come out was stunned silence.

WINKIE MA was born in Brooklyn, NY. She attended Stuyvesant High School in New York, NY, and Emory University in Atlanta, GA.

A Slight Misunderstanding

BY JOY SMITH, 2011

I wasn't doing anything out of the ordinary. I was just being Joy, being ten at a restaurant and heading to the bathroom. Normally my twin sister, Cherish, would have gone with me because we were always told "go with your sister," but for some reason I went alone.

I dressed how I felt comfortable, in what was my favorite thing at the time. Some girls wore jewelry or tutus. I was in love with my Sprewell jersey and Lee jeans. They were loose and fit with what the boys were wearing. I was a baller, and to complete my outfit I topped it off with my fitted hat that covered my zigzag braids, and headed for the bathroom.

What was I thinking? Nothing. It was a bathroom, of course other women would be in there, it was no big deal. Despite my attire, I was a girl and I had full access. As soon as I stepped one foot in the bathroom, a lady held her wet hands out as if to stop me and said, "Papi, you're in the wrong bathroom!"

"Huh?" I said.

Suddenly, I was confused and angry and of course embarrassed because, well, people were now looking at me. I was naïve, I realize now.

I was at that age where boys and girls were at the same height and my secondary characteristics hadn't developed yet, so it was easy to mistake me as a boy.

Still, a boy was the last thing I was. I didn't think I looked like a boy; besides, I had two earrings in my ear. Duh, boys don't wear two earrings, I thought to myself. As I sat back at the table upset and slightly embarrassed, I whined to my godmother that the lady thought I was a boy, and Spanish. She told me it was just a mistake, but I was furious. This lady needed her eyes checked, but then Cherish said, "You did it to yourself, Joy. STOP dressing like a boy and no one will think you're a boy. You're not a boy, Joy," she said angrily at me.

I wasn't the one she should be angry at. I was glaring at her. I wanted to burn a hole in her face. The lady already hurt my feelings; I didn't need her hurting mine too. Didn't anyone get that my feelings were bruised? This was a serious situation for me and no one was getting it or trying to make it better. And my own twin at that! She should be on my side. But this was a common statement with her. She always had something to say about my clothing. "Are you really going to wear that jersey again?" or, "Take that hat off."

From then on, I slowly stopped wearing my baller hoodies, fitted hats, and my prized jersey. I would never be mistaken again. Before my transformation was complete I was playing basketball with a group of boys, killing them, of course, when a boy asked:

"Are you a boy or a girl?"

I swooshed a three before telling him, "I'm a girl." I was never mistaken again.

JOY SMITH grew up in Arverne, Queens. She attended Brooklyn Community Arts and Media High School in Brooklyn, NY, and SUNY Oswego in Oswego, NY.

The Infamous Catcall

BY ROSEMARY ALFONSECA, 2016

"Hey beautiful, can I get your number?" is a familiar question I hear in the streets of my neighborhood. I'm walking to the train station when a stranger walks toward me trying to seem attractive, but he's failing miserably because his underwear is showing. He gives me that up-and-down stare that I hate more than anything. I'm being called beautiful, yet I feel anything but beautiful. He glares at my body and I can feel every goose bump on my skin. He doesn't get the hint that I'm beyond uncomfortable.

"Why are you ignoring me, beautiful?"

Here we go with the word "beautiful." I drop my gaze and try to ignore his inappropriate stare.

My first instinct always used to be to look down because I felt responsible. I used to be ashamed when men openly stared at me in public. But last year I decided to join the Sadie Nash Leadership Project, and now I see me, the world, and men differently.

I only joined the program so it would look good on my college resume, and when I found out it was just for girls, I wanted to run for the hills. During the first week of the program, we all felt awkward and shy with each other. But the following week our group leader, Leslie, instructed us to play a game called "Electric Fence." The fence was a rope attached to two walls. It was too high to get over easily, and we weren't allowed to go under it. All the girls had to help each other get over. We had to climb on each other's backs, hold hands, and trust that we would be caught on the other side. No matter what size we were, what language we spoke, or where we came from, we all came together to help each other get to the other side.

At the end of the exercise, we had all made it.

After this experience, I knew this program would benefit me. It got me to open up to people that I didn't know very well. What empowered me was when a young girl just like me shared her sexual assault story in our safe space. Every one of us was crying with her. It was like we all felt her pain. Everyone hugged her and was proud that she had been able to let it all out. I felt fortunate that she felt comfortable enough to share such a personal story with me and the others.

Soon after, we took a bus to a reproductive rights conference at Hampshire College. Women from all different states attend this conference once a year. When we arrived on campus we were starving, and they fed us nasty chili and cornbread. Luckily there were chocolate chip cookies, and that's all we ended up eating that night. But once the first event got going, it didn't matter to any of us. It was a gathering of women speaking out on abortion and telling their own personal stories. The audience was asked not to clap or talk but just to listen. I was sitting with some of my Sadie Nash friends, and we were all so touched by what we heard that all we could do was hold hands.

Before I found Sadie Nash, I thought it was normal to be sexually harassed in the streets of New York. Sadie Nash made me aware that catcalling is oppressive to me and other young women. I was inspired to accept my natural hair and stop chemically processing it. My mom said, "*Ese pelo tuyo es feo.*" Ever since I was young I felt like an outcast from my own home because my family had only one view on how hair should be: soft and straight. When I became part of this safe space of women, they showed me that there is no such thing as "good" hair. Not straightening my hair with chemicals is a symbol that not every woman of color has to accept this stigma. When women of color go natural, we are seen as "untamed" and "wild," but I want other women to join me in accepting our looks so that others will, too.

I don't want to be seen as just a "beautiful" girl anymore but rather a strong woman with a college degree and a future. I want every woman to find her own sisterhood, like I have.

I still don't like catcalling or being called "beautiful" by strange men, but it no longer makes me feel bad about myself. Sadie Nash has built my confidence and made me proud of who I am. I will begin to stare down the men who stare at me. They may want me to drop my gaze and lower my head, but I won't. I want to let them know that I see them and they no longer affect me.

I want to empower other young women to do the same.

ROSEMARY ALFONSECA was born in New York, NY. She attended the High School of Law and Public Service in New York, NY, and SUNY New Paltz in New Paltz, NY.

We Protest with Thunder, Not Lightning

BY SOLEDAD AGUILAR-COLON, 2017

It was like lightning. The bright flash of cameras was blinding as our adolescent faces appeared on their screens. We were seen but never really heard. We might as well have been silent. My friend and I walked hand in hand, my fingers tugging on hers. Turn right, I tugged her thumb, avoid the dog; turn left I tugged her pinky. *Avoid the book bags*, they whispered. My fingers clench around her slippery wrist. *Stop*, they say. I want to make sure she's okay, but her name slips from my tongue like raindrops and emerges into the puddle underneath our trembling feet. Ixchel reminded me of the Puerto Rican drink my grandmother makes during the holidays so she can drink away her ex-husband; her special eggnog with *un chin de rum*, we call it *coquito*. When I look at her hair, it's anything but the strong, independent black curls I had connected with the first moment we met. They were instead pressed down by the heavy pour of rain. They were straight for now, and the ends of her hair seemed to be held down by a hot-iron plank. They reminded me of prison bars. When I think of Ixchel and me, the color of our skins has never stood out so vividly; eggnog with a hint of rum fading away against the untouched snowflake white.

The voices of the protesters made noise but delivered no message as we marched with our soaking wet book bags toward the Trump Towers on Fifty-Sixth Street and Fifth Avenue. I jerk at the sound of a hundred geese screeching as it fills my eardrums, and I turn around to see a line of cars honking at the sight of our ostentatious signs that read, "Fuck Trump" and "Pussy Grabs Back." Puddles splash at our feet, causing teenagers to glance down at their wet, corporate American Apparel jeans in dread. They worried because the jeans cost fifty dollars, but never about how only ten dollars or less of that is given to the workers in China and India that make those jeans. They were protesting for the rights of working class people of color but never came to question how they are instead supporting the exploitation of people of color through their purchase of certain brands. The irony of leaving education to protest without being educated about what we were protesting. I thought of the abruptness of my decision to skip school because I had the ability to, but what if our education was our means of resistance? For Malala, she fought with a pen, paper, and books and was effective in generating change. We were uneducated protestors, so why protest at all?

I tap Ixchel on the shoulder to let her know of the instant publicity that the protest was attracting through the multiple snapchat videos and flashing cameras trained on our faces. Police officers were offering their hands to us and we walked across the street. Together. When we reached the Trump Towers, the officers put metal barricades around us. I soon realized they weren't corralling us; they were keeping everyone else out because, as newspapers would later write, this march of four hundred mostly privileged white students was peaceful. However, newspapers never deem protests as peaceful, so why us?

Six months earlier, I was filled with overwhelming pride as multiple fists ranging in colors from warm brown rice to sharp black pepper and spicy red curry rose in the air. The blood of our enslaved and undocumented ancestors, our history of broken backs and cracked feet spilled out on the clean "cookie-cutter" rugs of the New School building. I felt the shudder of the strong woman next to me as we breathed in and out as one, frightened of what was to come. We walked toward Grand Central Station with foreheads drenched in salty sweat and sticky lemonade fingers as red-faced men screamed "Sluts!" and "Put some clothes on!" Some mothers raised their fists in a salute to our anti-slut-shaming protest; others covered their daughters' eyes, shielding them from the free women of color fighting for their future. We didn't avert our eyes from the gaze of our zookeepers; we stared it in the face and unchained ourselves. At Grand Central Station, we screamed. We were thunder, demanding to be heard. A group of twenty women, hands linked in solidarity. Together we were no longer forced into their straightjackets that typecast us; we reclaimed a meaning that was inclusive of our power as young women of color. Cameras flashed and everyone stopped to admire the young women they thought belonged in zoos. Our skin glowed with all of the colors of the rainbow and every flag across the globe. Police officers just had to shut it down. Twenty cops, one for each of us, came down to tape our lips together, but we didn't need to speak in order to stand out. We were like thunder, no longer seen but heard. As the chief of the NYPD tells us that we were disturbing the peace and we have to leave in an orderly fashion, we stick up our middle fingers and chant, "We have nothing to lose but our chains."

SOLEDAD AGUILAR-COLON was born in the Bronx, NY. She attended Beacon High School in New York, NY.

It Is Me:
The Real Tianna C.

BY TIANNA COLEMAN, 2010

From the ages of thirteen to fifteen, I've been called an Oreo cookie. You know—black on the outside, white on the inside. People keep claiming that because I go to private school I'm a "white girl trapped in a black girl's body." This is because sometimes I speak with proper diction.

Many people think I'm spoiled because my school's tuition is over $6,000 and my guardians never miss a payment. They say I'm spoiled because both my parents are working in the court system and make a pretty good salary. Yet they'd never know that I grew up in the Edenwald Projects, that both my biological parents are deceased, and that I've witnessed over six deaths in my entire life and I'm only fifteen.

My mother died when I was five years old, from a stroke brought on by diabetes. I had to get used to having no mother and to having no father because he had to work most of my childhood. He would still have been working when my mother died, but he had an on-the-job accident and hurt his back and hip six years before he died. I was ten years old when he passed.

The first death I saw was my friend Jahmal getting hit by an eighteen-wheeler that wasn't even supposed to be on school grounds. Now, why it was on school grounds nobody knows. He was my best friend in the whole school, and he was only ten years old.

For as long I can remember, there were shoot-outs that I could always hear coming from the south side of the projects—I lived on the north side. I've witnessed enough during my years in Edenwald—a lot that was bad. So, when I finally have an opportunity to get away from this recklessness, you say I'm wrong?

Because I don't go to public school anymore and I've moved from the projects, people say I've "abandoned my community" and I've just moved up in society. I HATE THAT.

I did not abandon my community because I moved out of an apartment and into a private house. And I barely moved up in any society; I just left public school and went to Catholic school. I thought the community would be proud if one of us got out of the "ghetto" but I assume they all want us to stay with them because *they* can't get out.

I've left the projects, yes, but the projects NEVER left me. I love Edenwald; that's where I was born and raised! I'll never forget where I come from, and I never will forget just how far I've come. Yes, I'm in better living conditions, but it's still the Bronx. It's tough all over—so no one can say I'm "white on the inside" because I moved from Edenwald Projects to Edenwald Avenue.

I'm a proud African American girl; I love my culture, my people, and myself. I LOVE Edenwald, I'm still in Edenwald, and I always will be. Because at the end of the day, my family is Edenwald Projects and The Avenue! So, you will not call me an Oreo, because I am NOT an Oreo because last time I checked, a "spoiled brat" hasn't seen half of what I've seen.

TIANNA COLEMAN was born in Bronx, NY. She attended Academy of Mount St. Ursula in Bronx, NY, and the College of Southern Maryland in La Plata, MD.

She's a 7.8

BY SARAH KEARNS, 2017

I was waiting in line for a bagel, my hair standing on the back of my neck and my blood boiling. Two boys next to me had, with a laid-back cockiness, just scanned my body with their eyes.

"She's a 7.8."

They knew they were good-looking.

"I'd tap that."

It didn't matter to me.

"You should bang her, dude."

He should bang me. He should tap me. I'm a 7.8.

I've always been shy. I lacked the ability to speak up for myself. I let boys at school talk about the things that they wanted to do to my body. And I wouldn't say anything.

I'm too much of a pacifist. Or too weak. Either works. But this time, my fists were clenched and I was ready to punch. Maybe if I give them black eyes, I thought, they won't ever talk about a woman like that again.

I kept my fists held to my sides and I turned. They looked at me with sheepish smirks. I glared even harder.

"Chill. We were paying you a compliment."

He should tap that. I should chill. I'm a 7.8.

"What you said was disgusting. I'm a human being, not an object to fulfill your sexual desires."

I laughed. They stopped smiling. But I wasn't done yet.

I launched into a spiel. *"Feminism"* happened more than once. Also, *"Misogyny"* and *"The oversexualization of women."* I took my time. I got it out. I was soon out of breath but I was satisfied. I crossed my arms and gave them the same arrogant smirk they had given me. Here was the moment. What would they say?

"Sorry."

Sorry!

"We didn't know."

Like hell you didn't.

It wasn't much, but it was enough. For me, at least. They may have already forgotten that I answered back. But I haven't. And I won't.

I've changed. I always knew that men can say or do almost anything they want to a woman, without repercussions. So, it makes sense that they have no problem with the president grabbing at any woman he desires, Congress deciding who gets to decide, rating me.

These thoughts cloud my mind. A year ago, I was on the brink of losing hope. I thought feminism was a lost cause and that the only choice I had was to tolerate the way boys at my school spoke about my body. About me.

What changed? I found Girls Write Now. Suddenly, I had a community of loving, supportive women. They were strong. They made me want to be strong.

A year ago, I probably would've pretended not to hear my score on the bagel line. Not anymore. Women need to speak up. For one another and ourselves.

The cashier smiled at me warmly as she handed me my bagel. I thanked her as I walked past the two boys and to the door. They were silent. I felt strong.

SARAH KEARNS was born in Staten Island, NY. She attended Curtis High School in Staten Island, NY.

"Writing does not have to be done in total isolation. It can be fitted around the sides and in between, it can happen in the full throttle of family life or during periods of wild singledom. After cooking, during a bath, before work. And even better news—even when you're not actually doing it, you're still sort of doing it. Living is writing too, and, believe it or not, so is not writing. The typical fullness of a girl's life, of a woman's life, can certainly be a frustration, but it can also be a writer's greatest gift and opportunity. That gentleman in his garret doing nothing but writing often discovers he has little to write about. But the fifteen-year-old girl with school assignments and chores, Instagram and Twitter and crushes, and frenemies and family, and beauty regimes and sick days, might feel she doesn't have a moment, but what she's brewing inside her is writing too. And watch out when it comes to the boil."

—–ZADIE SMITH—–

Dinner Time

BY JOANNE LIN, 2011

The summer air wraps tight against the room. "How was your day?" Ma asks. Her voice drifts into the air and collides with the smell of rice. Chopsticks bang into one another. Soft words said as a battle for the last piece of broccoli emerges. Taste buds, they sway and dance. Stomachs dissolve into happiness, smiles erupt.

This love, rare as it is, stumbles and falls into an everyday routine.

JOANNE LIN grew up in Manhattan's Chinatown neighborhood. She attended Millennium High School in New York, NY, and the University at Albany, SUNY in Albany, NY.

Every Little Thing

BY CALAYAH HERON, 2014

It was back in the early 2000s, when everything seemed so simple; I was six or seven at the time, and my mother was still in her twenties. When I'd come home from school, she would be there in our small kitchen, still in her clothes from the night before, making rice and corned beef while talking on the phone. Bob Marley's "Buffalo Soldier" would be playing absently in the background, and the *sizzle sizzle* of meat cooking slowly in oil would accompany the mellow music. My stomach would growl vehemently when the smell of it hit my nose, and my mother would give me that knowing smile of hers when she heard it. Before settling down, we would greet each other with a hug and a kiss, and then I'd go into the living room to put my stuff away; the weight of the day would be shed with every outer layer of clothing I took off.

As I'd make my way back into the kitchen, I'd watch my mother continue to make our dinner and talk on the phone at the same time. I'd laugh at her silly antics of flailing her hands in wild gestures, trying to make a point to someone who couldn't even see her. Her high-pitched laugh always infected me with its cheeriness, even if I couldn't fully understand whatever joke was being told. Just the sound of her mirth gave me reason to smile. After she finished with what was to be our dinner, and her conversation had conveniently ended, we'd make our way into the bedroom to eat.

Once the door opened, the music would become louder in our ears, pumping from the speakers on the little radio that sat in the corner of the room. As I'd sit on the bed with my plate of food, my head would unconsciously rock back and forth, bringing my whole upper body with it as I swayed to the rhythm of the bass guitar, the sound of the islands moving through me.

There wouldn't be any conversation yet, just the King of Reggae filling our ears with his singing of war and survival. My childish mind couldn't really comprehend the true meaning behind the words, of course, so I'd just hum along to the lyrics, singing the words I knew. My mother would sing along with me, but somehow with more power behind her voice, and I'd be able to hear her heart.

It was when she would finish her food, and I'd hurry up to finish mine, that we'd go put away the dishes, and lie down on the mattress-made-futon. My mother would stroke my hair, fingers raking my scalp in a soothing manner, and hum a tune similar to the smooth melodies of *whoy yoy yoy* surrounding us. She'd ask me about school from time to time, pausing in her humming to speak up whenever a question struck her mind. With my belly being full and my hair being petted, I would close my eyes and answer just as softly. My mother would then get up and walk over to the radio, momentarily leaving me cold under the warm covers. The radio was always on her favorite reggae station; I liked to call it the "oldies station" because the songs that played were the songs she grew up with, and the feeling of nostalgia would engulf me whenever I heard them. She would turn down the volume until the music was just a low buzz in the background that had a nice, slow rhythm. She'd then get back on the bed, lift the covers, and wiggle back next to me before lying down on her back with her arms stretched on either side. I'd lay my head on one of her arms, usually the left one, and grab her other arm to wrap around my waist; by then I'd just be able to make out the words *Dreadlock Rasta, in the heart of America . . .*

My mind would start to think of everything and nothing as she went back to massaging my head. Thoughts would start to drift at such a fast pace, but I could hear them clearly, as if they were being read to me slowly. Why were we in such a small apartment? Why couldn't my little sister be with us, when she was just across the hall with her father? Why was he so mean? Why couldn't my mother kick *him* out? Didn't she wonder about these things too?

I would always think on those nights, maybe if my mother was a little stronger, or if my sister's father was a little nicer, then we'd be able to get my sister back and then she could listen to the oldies station, too. Instead, I was able to hear her father's new soundtrack blaring from next door on some nights. I felt as though my sister didn't really care for his music, but she was only a baby, so she couldn't pick sides. It wasn't fair that her father got to choose for her and my mother had no say. My mother didn't find that fair either, it seemed.

These thoughts that always lodged themselves into my brain, thoughts that usually made my eyes burn and my throat tighten, never took hold of me during that time, though, or any other time before or after. Just before my heart could clench and my stomach could drop as reality had started to creep up on me, the harsh reality of what was truly wrong with the picture that was our lives, my mother would wrap both arms around me and squeeze real tight, lifting her chin so I could fit my head into the crook of her neck. It was those moments when I liked to breathe in her scent. She always smelled of Johnson's Baby Oil because she loved their products and the way they left her skin feeling smooth. I liked it, too. The sound of her soft humming along to the music, and the secure feeling of her warm arms wrapped around me, always managed to put me to sleep. Reality would wait another day as I dreamed.

Woy yoy yoy, woy yoy-yoy yoy, Woy yoy yoy yoy, yoy yoy-yoy yoy!

CALAYAH HERON was born in the Bronx, NY. She attended Cardinal Spellman High School in the Bronx, NY, and Dickinson College in Carlisle, PA.

Growing Up Now

BY EBONY McNEILL, 2008

I was ten years old and I was in my grandma's room standing in front of the mirror looking at myself. I noticed that the left side of my chest was bigger than the right side of my chest. I started to get worried because I didn't know why it was like that. Then I just forgot all about it and started jumping on the bed and I started to twist and turn all around the bed. I heard my grandma yelling. She said *Ebony stop jumping on the bed before I spank your behind.* I jumped off of the bed and ran into the living room where my grandma was. I hopped up on the couch and started to jump. She said *Ebony stop jumping on the couch.* But I didn't listen. She said are you hard of hearing? I got off of the couch and lifted up my shirt and told her my left chest was bigger than the right one and I didn't know why it was like that. I told her I think something is wrong with me. She screamed *Oh my God, you're growing breasts. We have to go and get you a training bra.*

I put on my jacket and we walked to KidsTown on Nostrand Avenue. That was where you get the cheapest training bras from. While we were walking down the street she explained to me that breasts are a part of a female's body and that they only grow when you're a certain age. I was so embarrassed. I asked her why was she talking so loud out in public, and I told her I didn't want everyone to know my business. She said *Business, what business, you ain't got no business.* Then we walked into KidsTown. I went right to the training bras. I picked up a pink one with silver lace and a white one and another white one, but it had little pink flowers on it. I hurried up and paid for them then ran out of the store.

Back at home, I grabbed the pink one first and put it right on over my head. It felt soft but it was a little itchy. I felt very strange. It was weird. I couldn't believe I was growing breasts. As soon as I finished putting on the bra I went to my grandma. She looked at me and smiled and said *You're growing up now.* Then she called everyone she knew on the phone and said *Ebony has her first training bra!* I felt sick to my stomach.

EBONY McNEILL was born in Bed-Stuy, Brooklyn. She attended the Adolescent Employment and Education Program, Kingsborough Community College, and Brooklyn College in Brooklyn, NY.

Abandoned by Faith

BY LAURA ROSE CARDONA, 2017

"I love you. God bless you. Goodnight." A quick kiss on the cheek, adjusting my blanket so that I was properly tucked in before she smiled, turning away and exiting the room. This simple sentence of eight words has always been the staple of my mother's bedtime departure. It was as if she was so afraid that I would somehow slip away so deeply into a slumber that, for whatever reason, I would never awake again, and this blessing was the only way to guard against such a tragedy. I could not recall a single night in my life that this blessing was absent from our goodnights to each other. Even in the swells of our most stormy arguments, we would always manage to momentarily hold our anger beneath the rippled waters long enough to gaze upon each other and whisper the final words of the evening:

"I love you. God bless you. Goodnight."

Always, without fail, until one day, the angers suffocating within the waters beneath us rose above my mother, choking her with such fury that she was, for the first time, unable to deliver her faithful blessing, and I was alone, unprotected in the night.

Although I wasn't entirely alone. There was a man, or at least the image of a man—as the scripture goes—who had, for my entire life,

followed me, shadowing my every move. This figure was God. Our relationship was like that of a boat in rugged waters. Sometimes, like when
I was just a little girl, I was sure he was there behind me, serving as my
protector and guide. However, as I began to mature in my teenage years,
my faith wavered.

I recall lying on my bed when I was only twelve years old, my body
curled into a C-shape as I held my pillow near my chest. I was in bed later
than I should have been, all because I had just wrapped up a near six-
hour conversation with a friend at my middle school. Even though we
were no longer on the phone together, I wondered why her voice still
echoed through my mind, preventing me from sleep.

I began reminiscing about all the moments we had shared up to this
point. The first time I spoke to her was when she dropped her sharp-
ener on the ground and I, feeling compelled to help her, crawled on all
fours across the classroom tiles to retrieve it for her. She would message
me during class, despite the fact that she sat only a few rows away from
me, and I would respond without hesitation or thought. Once I plucked
a flower from its stem in the botanical hall of the Bronx Zoo to present
to her as a makeshift present, only to flee the zoo in screams as a bee I
disturbed vowed revenge on me. I remembered all this and more, and
it played in my mind like a projector, almost mockingly, laminating my
many failed attempts to capture her attention. My affection poured
like a pipe that had been busted and was spewing water, except this
pipe was more like an artery streamlining from my heart, and the
liquid was nothing but love, and that's when I realized: I was in love
with her.

Such a simple thought sent my mind awry. How could I love someone
of the same sex? How could God let this happen to me? At the very least,
Eve had the choice of choosing the apple, but here I was, performing for
an operating theater, strapped to a medical table, the apple of lust gagged
my mouth, while the devil grinned above me, wasting no time in bringing his surgical knife down, extracting God from my heart and my heart
from my God.

The hole carved within me by Satan burned with passion. I set out to fill the void with love—or was it lust? What did I care at this point? Like a bride on her wedding day, the scriptures abandoned me, left me in solitude at the altar with nothing but the vows of the Bible to accompany me, except now the parchment was just a painful reminder of what we could have been together. So, I averted my attention to the bridesmaid. Every girl that circled me was a target that I could thrust my naïveté upon, desperately trying to claw some sense of my sexuality out from the fog of rejection and denial. Yet no matter how much I thirsted for attention, the hole within me did not sprout with life. It seemed the rains of sorrow made no-good fertilizer, and the flames of desire did little to quell its cold.

So, I sat at that altar, wondering where was my groom, wondering why my parents didn't walk me down this aisle of pity, but most of all, wondering why my mother no longer uttered: "I love you. God bless you. Goodnight."

LAURA ROSE CARDONA was born in Brooklyn, NY. She attended Williamsburg Preparatory High School in Brooklyn, NY, and The King's College in New York, NY.

Red Apple Pie

BY MICHAELA BURNS, 2010

The wooden-plank floor with faded basketball markings is where my mother, adorned in a beanie, the black and gold of the McUpton Tigers and the same toothy smile as my own, posed with other cheerleaders for a picture which now lives in a gold frame on top of the television in my grandmother's living room. Eyeing the stage at the other end of the room, I imagined seeing my mother, and the two other members of her singing group, the Teardrops, in long, sky-colored dresses and loose, flowing hair newly freed from their standard style of tightly woven braids. The story of the talent competition I'd heard many times. The eleven-year-old threesome sang "My Guy" by Mary Wells and popped their fingers rhythmically to the driving beat while their arms, from the elbow down, swayed back and forth in unison like windshield wipers. The well-worn story always ended with a description of how the thunderous applause seemed to rock the room and how, most importantly, Grandmamma stretched her stained lips in a smile from ear to ear. Always missing from the story is who won. My own journey to this worn space alive with ghosts insistent on telling stories began two weeks earlier.

Grandmamma and I sat across from each other, our eyes focused on the task—peeling the red apples for Red Apple Pie. Dark red peels formed slow, continuous circles inside the faded silver bowl positioned on the kitchen table. A vessel brought back from a long-ago trip to Mexico overflowed with plump, blushing apples. The Kentucky air found its way leisurely through the screened windows of the kitchen, along with the familiar sound of buzzing insects.

A dull knife clenched in my small fist carved off the thick shells of the fruit. At ten years of age, it was thought that I could only be trusted with a knife so dull that it might as well have come out of my plastic kitchen set I received for Christmas three years ago. The only difference between my plastic cutlery and my current knife was that my doll's knife was pink and probably sharper. Despite this obstacle and my lack of experience in the kitchen, I was eager to see that quiet, approving look my grandmother wore when a job had been done well.

Grandmamma looked up from her own decreasing pile of apples, blinking thick curly lashes. I looked into her freckled face and shook my head affirmatively. She peered into my half-empty bowl of apples that I had hacked mercilessly. Half of the tender white flesh still stubbornly clung to the peel.

She clicked her tongue to the rhythm of the cricket hovering outside the window, before letting loose her laughter.

"Child, you sure know how to murder an apple."

Putting her experienced, wrinkled hand over mine, she guided it to the top of the fruit. Together, we sliced horizontally around the circumference until perfect circlets filled the bowl. Gazing at our accomplishment, we burst into laughter like girlfriends sharing a special secret.

"This is how you do it," Grandmamma said, as she turned her naturally bright eyes toward me and gave me her nod of approval.

MICHAELA BURNS grew up in Manhattan, NY. She attended Calhoun School in New York, NY, and Johns Hopkins University in Baltimore, MD.

It Rained Last Night

BY YESENIA TORRES, 2012

It rained last night.

It was quiet while the wind blew through my open window. Death filled my nostrils as I slept, but my senses didn't prepare me for the morning's Facebook posts. Three of my friends had posted that your soul passed away in the dark, whispering goodbye to the world that used to be beneath your feet. I could barely believe it. I thought it was a messed-up joke waiting to unfold, and I just wanted to be told what really happened to you.

While in my first-period class that morning, rumors of your passing played in our ears, our minds repeated, "Why?" I counted the seconds into minutes until the rustling of the loudspeaker awoke with Sister Elizabeth's weary voice: "I am glad to see each and every one of you today . . ." each word spoken with force. Our senior class was then told to report to the auditorium. As we walked down the aisles to the empty seats that awaited us, I never felt such a paralyzing silence. I wondered if we were ready to hear what would come next. I sat in the cold chair while scanning the faces of the faculty members standing before us. Some already had traces of tears in their empathetic eyes. Our principal spoke: "I'm sure you all undoubtedly know that one of your classmates passed away." The pain left me speechless.

The next two days became a blur. I sat in English class staring at your empty chair expecting you to simply walk into the room and take your place, apologizing for being late. I made excuses for you when I barely knew you. Why did you do it? Was life not worth it? Or were you trying too hard to be perfect? I sat, wishing time had a reverse button so I could turn back to Monday and tell you everything would be all right.

But now it's Friday, October 21, 2011. Sitting in one of the already-filled rooms at the funeral parlor, I am dressed in black. Mourners surround me, letting their sorrows overwhelm me, causing these sympathetic tears to run down my cheeks. And there you are in your suit, your beautifully brown skin turned pale. Blood-red rose petals engulf you as we whisper prayers, hoping your eyes will open. Your brother and sister continue to speak at the podium, letting their words cram the stifling air. They mention your smile from ear to ear, your stories, your jokes, and your powerful laugh. I envy their memories of you.

Because the only memory that burns in my head is your lifeless body hanging from a tree.

YESENIA TORRES was born in New York, NY. She attended Christ the King Regional High School, Queens, NY, and SUNY Oswego in Oswego, NY.

Loving in New Ways

BY AVA NADEL, 2013

"¿Cuantos años tienes tú, Norma?"

"Dos."

Dos? I thought. *That's odd. Norma had to be older than sixteen.* Later that night, after dinner, my homestay mother told me that Norma has an intellectual disability: she is twenty-eight and doesn't know how to read or write.

Because my Spanish wasn't entirely perfect, I was unsure of how I should go about communicating with Norma. I had tried conversing with her using my Spanish, but even then, she seemed not to understand basic phrases I was saying. So, I sat there, at the dining table, shelling the lima beans for dinner. I could feel her staring at me, smiling as I plopped the shelled beans into a bowl. She then stuck one of them in front of my face. I had put the unshelled lima bean into the bowl with the shelled ones. She started laughing both with her mouth and eyes, and I did the same. We may not have been communicating using words, but using our emotions was enough.

For the next four days, I didn't feel so nervous around Norma anymore. I found that just by smiling and laughing, we could read each other's minds just fine. The next few mornings, I would be applying sunscreen in the bedroom and she'd come in, freshly showered, combing her silky, long black hair. We'd sit there in silence, taking care of ourselves separately, but fully aware of the other's presence. Much as I had when peeling the lima beans, I found that if I pulled off humorous actions, we'd improve our communication. I would play around with the stray dogs and cats and have her try and throw food in my mouth. One way or another she'd burst into a fit of giggles.

Through forming this sisterly bond with Norma with hardly any speaking, I learned perhaps one of the most valuable life lessons that any teenager could learn at my age: relationships don't need to be built on much. Norma and I surrounded each other with smiles and laughter and I came to realize that positive energy and emotions were all we needed.

The last morning of my homestay, my homestay mother, Carmela, was cooking us breakfast. Norma turned up the radio, humming along to what I assumed was her favorite song. She took me by the hands and started dancing with me. I could feel the tears welling up in my eyes— the tears I refused to let fall because I knew that if I showed her how weak I was, I wouldn't be able to explain it.

I miss her. I miss her cooing at the stray cat underneath the dining table. I miss her combing her wet hair as she watched me spray sunscreen on my mosquito bites before I left to weed the garden. I miss the dimples in her cheeks from when she'd get herself into a fit of giggles and couldn't stop laughing.

Sometimes the best love is the one that can exist without words.

AVA NADEL was born in New York, NY. She attended Millennium High School in New York, NY, and Guilford College in Greensboro, NC.

Inspiration from My Mother

BY FANTA CAMARA, 2013

I am from Guinea, a small country located in West Africa. In Guinea, elders believe that marriage is more important than education. They believe that education can only be important at certain points in one's life. They also believe that marriage is a symbol of dignity and an honor to the family. While in school at the age of sixteen, my mother was a very smart girl. Her teachers never complained about her academic performance. But her parents took her out of school to get her married to my father. Although marriage was the last thing on my mother's mind, she was never given the chance to choose between her education and marriage. She married my father, whose family promised that she would continue her education.

After getting married to my father, she did not go to school again due to some financial problems in the family. Instead, my mother started to do business at the marketplace in her neighborhood. At that time, she was not happy. After six years of marriage, she realized that only education could help her get where she wanted to be, so she went back to school and became a nurse. Going back to school did not only change her life, but it changed her children's lives as well. Watching my mother struggle, I realized that education is what will help me get to the top of the mountain. I believe in education and I will do all I can to make sure I get my degree.

Does history repeat itself, or do people allow it to repeat? I know that my mother suffered a lot, but I will not let the same thing happen to me. My mother is the person who had the biggest influence on me. My mother is my history, my present, and future. The only history that I will allow to repeat is the one that bettered my mother's life, which was getting an education. Even though everything in her life gave her the right to give up on her dreams, she never did. She fought for her children and herself. Thinking about her reminds me of the many responsibilities I have in my life.

One year ago, I received a call from my grandmother. It was very strange because the communication between my grandmother and me decreased a lot when I came to the United States. She wanted me to marry someone she had chosen for me. I thought about what happened to my mother being married at such a young age. My mother's struggles and living in the United States made me stronger and helped me realize that the decision is mine. No one can force me to get married.

I am pursuing my education because I am the leader of my life. I chose to go to college and make my mother proud of me. I choose to be educated.

FANTA CAMARA was born in Conakry, Guinea. She attended Bronx International High School in Bronx, NY, and the University at Albany, SUNY in Albany, NY.

Mother

JENNIFER LEE, 2016

I.

"My mother crossed an ocean for more power." This is what I say on the angry days, when I think of my mother crossing the Pacific to come study in America, stripping me of the language of my ancestors and bringing me to a country I cannot call my own. But then I remember who that power was for, and I think I am being little too heartless. I say instead: "My mother crossed an ocean for me."

This is how I first remember my mother: I am four, and she is visiting my classroom for parent-observation day. The teacher calls my mother "Mrs. Lee." My mother does not correct her. I want to take her by the shoulders and shake her, ask, *Why don't you tell her that your last name is Kim, K-I-M, 김 in Hangul, 金김 in Hanja?* Instead, I learn not to correct the teacher; never speak up in the classroom—the teacher is always right.

We move to the city in second grade; in third, my mother packs up to leave. "It's all your fault," she tells my father. "It's all your fault," she tells my father. It's all your fault; It's all your fault; 다 너탓이야; I hate you and I hate you and I hate you. She has been alternating between spending a month in the city and a month in New Hampshire, back and forth, back and forth, studying for her PhD. This time, she says she wants to leave forever, and I want to draw the words back into her mouth, grab them from the air, apologize for her a thousand times and tell my father "She didn't mean it; She doesn't mean it; She never means what she says; She never says what she means."

My mother is in New Hampshire when my father is arrested; silence blankets our family like snow; winter has never been quieter. I imagine she wants to tell my father *I trusted you to look after our kids*; 어떻게 이럴 수 있어; *how could you do something like this*, but she says nothing when he comes home. That year she finally finishes her dissertation; she comes back home to stay when I am in fifth grade.

Once, my sister said to my mother, "I don't want to be a housewife when I grow up. I'm going to get a job. I'm going to be better than you." My mother said nothing; she ladled sweet potato curry into my sister's bowl. I wanted to take her by the shoulders and shake her, ask, *Why don't you tell her that you do have a job, that the only reason why you work from home is because you have to take her to school every day, that with a PhD from Dartmouth in computer science you could be getting a real job outside of the house, that if Milkman was right in saying that 'Wanna fly, you got to give up the shit that weighs you down,' then we are the ones weighing you down?* I say nothing; my sister begins eating; I think, *Maybe my mother wants my sister to do better, too.*

I am on the 7 train, talking to a girl I just met at a writing workshop. She is Chinese; she moved to America two years ago. She stares out the window as she says, "When I lived in China, I knew what I wanted to be: a doctor. But now I'm here, and don't know; I'm lost. Sometimes I regret coming to this country." Her bangs hug her glasses, and I imagine she could be a younger version of my mother; I realize I have never seen photos of my mother from before she married, that I do not know what she looked like before I was born. I wonder if this is how my mother feels in America: lost. I wonder what she wanted to be in high school. I wonder if she regrets coming to this country. I wonder what she looked like in high school. I wonder if she regrets my being born.

My sister and I are eating curry again for dinner when my mother says, "If I leave, know that it was your fault." I wonder what she means by leave—leave as in leave the city, leave as in leave the country, or leave as in die, as in, *There is nothing for me here, but there is nothing for me elsewhere, either.* She goes on to say, "너 때문에 참고 있다"—that is, *I am putting up because of you,* or *I am enduring because of you.* I wonder what it is she is putting up with—my father, or the loneliness of working at home, or maybe the unbearable weight of not being heard.

As much as I may say that my mother crossed the Pacific for more power, I think maybe I am just lying to myself. I do not know why my mother came to this country, or what she was running from; all I know is that what she found was not what she was looking for. I try to remind myself of that when I think of what it would be like to return to Korea— that my imagined homeland, too, may be nothing but a utopia: "u-" as in "no," and "-topi" as in "place."

II .

ni hao

你好。囝

annyeonghaseyo

안녕하세요! ㅇㅂㅇ

Hi. :)

¡Hola! ñ_ñ

zhai zuo sum ma

在做什麼?

jiguem mwo haeyo

지금 뭐 해요?

Just staying low. . __ .

Si, si.

wo yi jin gao shu ni

我已經告訴你 —

nol-i gaja

놀이 가자!

I don't want to fall.

¡Cualquier cosa que quieren es bueno!

wo bu yao

我不要.

wae yo jebal a

왜요?? 제발, 아? ㅠㅅㅠ

Aww.);

¡Dios mío, vamos a alegrar esta cara preciosa!

ni men yao zuo sum ma jui zuo ba

你們要做什麼 就做吧.

ya-ho u-ri mal no-eul-kka-yo

야호! 우리 말 놓을까요?

JENNIFER LEE was born in New Haven, CT. She attended Hunter College High School and Columbia University in New York, NY.

En Su Espejo

BY LUNA ROJAS, 2017

The first time I visited a college campus, I was six years old. I was there for my mother, not for me—or so I thought.

My mother, a first-generation Latina and single parent, walked into her economics class at a New York City college full of ambition and eagerness, with me in tow. She told me to read and say nothing until class was over. I took quick peeks at my mother, noticing how different she looked in the classroom. Eyes forward, hair up, she scribbled notes on everything the professor said. For the first time, she was devoting all her attention and focus to something that wasn't me. I felt jealous. I didn't understand my mother's drive to finish college back then, because I hadn't yet learned to see past myself.

Growing up, my mother fell prey to a common trap for children of immigrants—particularly women. Driven to provide for herself and help support her parents, she began working as soon as she graduated from high school, planning to attend college at the same time. But as a girl in a Latino household with traditional ideas about gender, she wasn't encouraged to continue her education. Meanwhile, her parents constantly urged her brother to think big, telling him that he could become a teacher, doctor, or lawyer. And so my mom was disadvantaged early on, because she was never taught to prioritize her own education. Soon she stopped going to school to focus on work.

After I was born, my mother realized she had to go back to school to support us both. It was a long process, with multiple stops and starts. She spent a year in school when I was six, then left again to be more present in my life. Then, as I began high school, she went back to academia again, determined to finish her degree by taking one class a semester. And although I still missed my mom, I was finally old enough to understand what she was teaching my brother and me.

Over time, watching my mother balance school and her job made me adopt a similarly serious work ethic. My final year in high school often made me fantasize about extending the twenty-four-hour day by a few hours or so. An average day consisted of high school and a sociology course at City Technology College, after which I would do a 360, transforming into a sparkling sales associate at Banana Republic for the remainder of my evening. As a food-service worker, I also experienced what it was like to wash dishes for pay, then come home to wash even more. I babysat and cleaned other people's homes, and took orders from hangry customers—sometimes feeling more like a menu than a person.

During the last few weeks of my final semester in high school, I was so busy that I worried exclusively about myself, feeling that I'd taken on too much. Then I caught sight of my mother up late, making flash cards, and realized she had been doing everything I had—and much more—throughout my teenage years. In no way could I compare my hard work to hers. She didn't have the luxury to worry exclusively about herself. In that moment, I remembered the lunches she had packed for me every day, the snacks and inspirational texts she'd sent when I felt overwhelmed, and how the question "How was your day, honey?" never failed to come out of her mouth, no matter how tired or busy she might be.

Adulthood begins when you are able to look beyond the person you see in the mirror. Now, as I get ready to go to college, I know how much I owe to my mom. Watching her strive to complete her degree while raising kids and holding down a full-time job helped me understand the true value of a good education, and showed me that balancing work and study—while difficult—could be done.

My mother's drive came from her own confrontation with the realities of adulthood and motherhood. When she took me to that economics class years ago, she was learning to look away from the person in the mirror and toward the child who stood beside her. Now, as I look forward to beginning college this fall, I know that I do it for myself as well as my mother—who has done nothing short of everything to get me here.

LUNA ROJAS was born in New York, NY. She attended Cobble Hill High School and the Pratt Institute in Brooklyn, NY.

Diamonds

BY JULEISY POLANCO, 2017

Today my mother got me diamond earrings as a graduation gift. Today is February 22, not June 23. She was so excited she could not wait. She kept saying things like, "Don't lose them, they're expensive . . . diamonds are a girl's best friend," while I read the message she wrote on the box: "To Juleisy, from Mami, this is your graduation gift. You deserve it for all your hard work."

I wish I could say my excitement matched hers. I would never buy myself expensive *things* like that. I admit it: I love diamonds. But for me, they are symbols to be admired, not objects to be worn and shown off. I wonder if my mom would have been as excited if she had known that what I really want is a diamond tattoo right in the middle of my chest.

This gem has many dimensions, like the sides of an argument or chapters of a story. Their qualities make them rare and desirable prizes that everyone wants but few will ever have. Men have risked their lives to mine these stones. People have stolen, killed, cheated, and lied to get their hands on the wealth associated with them. I know that greed is the driving force that has made so many willing to put aside their own morality to fill the void that comes from wanting. I know that my ancestors have been beaten and enslaved in pursuit of diamonds, and that in many countries this abuse continues.

Because of this, *every* diamond, even the ones in the earrings my mother gave me, represents great sacrifice. Maybe it is because of the sacrifice that we put these stones on such a high pedestal. That is raw. I want to wear that on my chest. I want to show the world that I think of my own values as jewels, equivalent to the biggest or brightest diamond there is.

The process behind this beautiful product is what intrigues me. It can take more than three billion years of heat, pressure, and darkness for diamonds to form. That is almost as old as the earth. When they are first dug up, diamond roughs do not look very appealing. Only with molding and shaping and careful cutting do they become the gems people find so desirable, bright, transparent, reflective.

The word "diamond" comes from the Greek, meaning "untamed, unbreakable, unalterable." Not all diamonds have the same qualities, however, and only those with the fewest impurities—the finest color and greatest clarity—are suitable for jewelry. But beauty is not the only thing that gives a diamond value. Diamonds are so hard they are almost indestructible, so not only do they shine brighter than all other stones, they are hard enough to cut through any one of them. This makes them very useful in manufacturing and industry. Diamonds can sparkle in rings and necklaces AND do the unglamorous work of cutting, drilling and grinding. How amazing would it be to marry both these qualities within ourselves?

With my tattoo, I hope to be branding myself with a different perspective on diamonds. It won't cost as much as the real thing, and I will not have to take special care of it or be afraid of losing it, but it will be the image of a valuable object I carry with me at all times. I want it in the center of my chest because that is the place from which my diamond roughs will be mined. This image will project my strength, signify that my values are unalterable, and show how close to my heart I hold my worth. Like a diamond, I hope to endure the pressures and darkness ahead to become a strong and valuable woman in my family and community. I hope to share my own light and also to reflect the light around me.

When people see my tattoo, I expect they will have questions about my choice. If they ask, I will tell them that my diamond symbolizes all the qualities I want to have: strength, resistance, transparency, and brilliance. I hope it raises questions about their own choices as well.

JULEISY POLANCO was born in the Bronx, NY. She attended Bronx Studio School for Writers and Artists in Bronx, NY, and SUNY New Paltz in New Paltz, NY.

Baby Things

BY EMELY PAULINO, 2010

My nose crinkled as I opened the closet door; the smell of old paper and crayons consumed me. With a sigh, I heaved a basket labeled "Emely Photos" that was filled to the top with albums from my first birthday, vacations in the Dominican Republic, or trips to the park. Outside I could hear my father talking to the moving-truck driver about how horrible the Mets' last season was. Across the hall I could hear my mom's voice as she sang along to Spanish radio. I opened a suitcase that had several baby dresses, socks, and toys. They all gave off a slight aroma of baby powder.

"Ma, why do you keep all this?" I asked her, as she came down the hallway.

"Because they're your baby things. When you get older, you're going to look back at this and smile."

One by one, I picked up my baby things—a frilly pink dress, one-piece PJs, booties. "But if we're moving, Ma, won't this just take up space?" I said, shaking my head. Underneath all the infant clothing, I picked up something I hadn't looked at for a while.

"Remember when you wrote that, Emely? It was your first story," she said to me. I flipped through the pages of "Alex the Puppy," a story about a lost dog, written on jumbo Post-its. After so many years, the purple marker in which the words were written was fading. Next to the Post-its was the stuffed puppy that inspired my first story. Outside, I could hear the thud of boxes being placed into the truck.

"Emely, bring your boxes. We're loading up the truck!" my dad called out to me. Briefly, I flipped through the book for the last time, repacked the suitcase, and walked down the steps to the driveway. Next to my baby things was the box that had all my books—Kafka, Márquez, Díaz, and notebooks filled with story outlines and poems showing just how much I've grown.

EMELY PAULINO grew up in Queens, NY. She attended The Young Women's Leadership School of Astoria in Queens, NY, and Bard College in Annandale-on-Hudson, NY.

"Writing is not just about what we want to say, but about who will be there to listen and respond to our words. When we are stuck and struggling with a blank page, often the best medicine is to get up from our desks and go out and listen to other people. Grow your family of fellow writers and kindred spirits. Reward your hard work with community and connection."

--MIA ALVAR--

Chinese Food on My Chapped Lips

BY LUCY TAN, 2011

The hollow space below my soles set my feet free and my sandals hung off my ankles by their Velcro straps. I was little, I thought. My legs swung back and forth aimlessly, hoping but not wanting to reach something unknown in the void below the round table. I flailed my loose, bare arms around and placed them on the shoulders of the two people next to me. On the left was my father, with his elbows resting on the edge of the table and on the right, my mother, devouring the food that streamed toward us with the help of waiters running like worker ants.

I didn't want to eat the mysterious food put upon the table. I stared at the china saucer before me; for such a small dish, it held blotches of a venomous substance—bright yellow, shocking red, sickly green clumps of what could possibly be mistaken for the piercing eyes of poison tree frogs. Nanny leaned her elbows upon the edge of the table and Cousin Andy played with the tablecloth. There came a rumble and bump, as the dishes wobbled in place. Murky puddles of soy sauce trembled in place around pieces of roasted duck the same way I trembled from the uneven bursts of icy restaurant air-conditioning.

I'm ungrateful, too ungrateful. "The Lightning God will strike you one day," my grandmother professes. There is no such thing as the Lightning God. "Disobedient child!" I swallow the soggy mushrooms and the nights pass, as they always do, with the stars above as witness to what ill acts I've committed.

I placed these things in my stomach mindlessly. It was a duty to please my mother, my father, and my grandmother, due to the hard work and perspiration my grandmother expends for two hours every night, mixing and matching various groceries from the refrigerator, feeling the rising steam on her carved face. I was little and the world ended at the edges of my daily routines. I did not have plans; I was dependent and always at the command of others.

The reluctance of obeying duties gradually began to strike me. It lived in my gut, and every time I seemed to enjoy the food I was devouring, a part of me knew that eating was not pleasurable.

Eighth grade, the year before high school started, was the last year I had any spare rooms in me. Slowly, but surely, all the rooms became inundated by visitors, some staying longer than others, but all in constant demand for some part of me. They rented my taste buds, my throat, my stomach, and eventually when they needed every square inch, the only guest they allowed in was wind for airing out their rooms.

Now, looking at myself in storefront windows, I see someone running from one place to another, always too busy, too wary of wasting minutes of my time on unnecessary ventures. Food, whenever eaten, is often distasteful and seems to only be a means of comforting grumbles; the air rushing into my stomach from my fast-paced life, burning my esophagus, is often enough.

With Chinese food on my chapped lips, I rush out of my house to greet the world.

LUCY TAN was born in Brooklyn, NY. She attended Stuyvesant High School in New York, NY, and Case Western Reserve University in Cleveland, OH.

Write.

BY JANAE LOWE, 2015

I like to write because it is a way to express my feelings. When people read my writing, I want them to feel joy and to know who I really am.

People say that I am a funny, happy person but I don't see it. When people read my writing they always laugh. I don't write often but I write to relax my mind. I am a busy person and a lot goes through my mind. I want people to see the breakthrough I have experienced.

Overcoming the death of my grandmother was very hard because it took a lot of energy out of me. After she died, I started writing more. It felt good to reflect on my writing, with the smell of the ink of the pen and fresh paper. Using ink and paper relaxes me—it helps me calm down. It helps me to be able to write what I wish I could tell her so I feel that I can still communicate with her. It also helps me think about the good things that happened between me and her rather than her death. Writing gives me that wonderful feeling that I am creating something beautiful.

JANAE LOWE was born in the Bronx, NY. She attended High School of Economics and Finance in the New York, NY, and North Carolina Agricultural and Technical State University in Greensboro, NC.

Rising

BY EMILY DEL CARMEN RAMIREZ, 2013

"Uno, dos, y tres . . ." My father jumps off of the cliff into El Yaque del Norte, with me holding tightly onto his back. My arms tighten around his shoulders as I clasp my hands together.

"Agárrate mi muñeca!" Hold on my baby girl! he yells. I shut my eyes and bury my face in his back. He strengthens his grasp around my ankles, reaffirming my safety. We plunge into the water at full speed. Holding my breath, I open my eyes and he lets me go. The hairs on my arms stand. From twenty feet under, I see the shadows of my family members—*Abuela, Tío, Tía,* Mami, and my nine-year-old brother, Giovanny—waiting for me to surface.

In my country, La República Dominicana, learning to swim is a child's rite of passage, much like an older girl's *quinceañera*. Swimming marks the beginning of the road to independence for a child, just as a fifteen-year-old girl donning her first pair of high heels marks the beginning of womanhood. Today is my time to shine. It is my second baptism, the day that I must emerge from the water all by myself.

Still underwater, I look at my father's aqua-tinted image as he mouths the word *"Ve"* *Go.* A torrent of air bubbles escapes from his mouth. I frantically move my arms and legs, trying to swim up. I watch as he ascends from the water, leaving me to fend for myself.

I begin to panic and slowly sink. My arms and legs flail. The water rushes into my mouth as I gasp for air and all of the sudden, everything turns black. My father carries me to safety and I cough continuously, spitting water on the riverside.

Ten years later I am back at El Yaque del Norte. As I stand atop the cliff, the memories rush back to me. I remember my father's abandonment underwater, my rite of passage to independence. With one fell swoop, I again jump off the cliff in Jarabacoa, diving headfirst into the river. From twenty feet under, I see my mother and brother, waiting for me to rise.

I remember the moment my father walked out the door to our apartment six years ago—stark feelings of abandonment. I kick profusely at the water beneath me. I put up a fight against the malevolent water and its attempts to swallow me. I do not relent. I protest its attempts to envelop me, just as I struggled to stay afloat after my father's departure. Although my father's absence put more hours on my mother's work schedule and catalyzed my brother's rejection of an education, it motivated me to work hard—to aspire to becoming a foreign correspondent reporting on human rights abuses around the world.

I realize that my own plight has inspired me to be a voice for the voiceless.

Because now I have a voice:

I am Malala Yousafzai, yelling as the bullet hits me—demanding education for the women of Pakistan.

I am Pussy Riot, banging on the metal bars of the cell—demanding for the right to speak out.

I am a girl from the Congo, begging for an end to rape, torture, and female mutilation—yearning for respect.

I rise to the top and begin to tread water.

EMILY DEL CARMEN RAMIREZ was born in New York, NY. She attended Brooklyn Technical High School in Brooklyn, NY, and SUNY Geneseo in Geneseo, NY.

Joyful

BY ANGLORY MOREL, 2017

In the Morel house, Christmas was no joke. The smell of pine filled the air. The aroma of roasted chicken escaped the kitchen, where the counter overflowed with delicious treats for our house guests.

Our small NYC apartment located on the second floor of a thousand-year-old building felt tight. We all paced back and forth in the kitchen, in the living room, and in the bedroom making sure everything looked presentable. *"Anglory, guarda tus zapatos y ayúdame a recoger,"* my mother yelled as she gestured toward the shoes lying against the Christmas tree.

The Christmas tree—what a sight! Overstuffed with decorations. It was tall, too tall for our small apartment. It scraped the ceiling and covered half the wall. Adorned with huge glass balls of all colors, the huge pine tree was more decorated than the Macy's tree or even the Rockefeller skyscraping tree.

A buzz filled the room. They were here! Our guests made their way up the marble stairs and toward our door decorated with wrapping paper. Soon they would see all the green, red, gold, and silver hanging from every corner of our small space. A grin overtook my face. A little piece of home was coming to visit. Our beloved family, a reminder of the life we left back home on La Quisqueya, was at our doorstep.

Every year it was the same. We watched as people from all over the world, of different religions, races, and ethnicities, came together to be with their families in a land where differences were accepted and celebrated. Every year my cousins would call to tell me how happy they were to visit the United States, how lucky I am to live here, how many opportunities I have, how everyone from everywhere wants to be here. Christmastime was when we got to mix the love and culture from our little Caribbean island with the rush and buzz of New York City. We celebrated coming to this free country of hope and promise. Once a year we had the opportunity to see the ones who weren't as fortunate, to share this diverse land with them. At Christmas, joy filled every corner of the city and excitement raced in our hearts as we waited for them to make their way to us.

The door flew open and there they were, the family we all missed and loved. My eyes were set on one particular person, Ken Morel, my cousin, a caramel-colored boy whose facial hair was beginning to grow above his upper lip. His hat was way too big and sat awkwardly on his head. He was much taller than the last time I had seen him. I bet he could reach the star on the tree without even fully stretching his arms out. As soon as his eyes met mine, he let go of his luggage and rushed toward me. Memories of going to school with him and riding bikes flashed through my mind as we hugged. I stood back and admired my beautiful family. They only came once a year and now they were here. The thrill of seeing them melted like Christmas snow into pure joy, the joy that only they could bring me. *Feliz Navidad!*

ANGLORY MOREL was born in Santo Domingo, Dominican Republic. She attended Princeton University in Princeton, NJ.

Happiness in Compensations

BY BUSHRA MIAH, 2014

Before writing this piece, I met with my therapist and we spoke about the topic that lives deep in my soul, clouds my world, and secretly serves as the motive behind any major decisions I make. Within seconds of our conversation, tears began rolling down my cheeks and I could no longer handle the topic, in fear that talking about it would emotionally flatten me. And with this, I knew I had to write.

I was sitting at the dinner table, silently chewing my food, while my father sat to my left, speaking about his latest experience on the A train. Observing my nearly empty plate, he reached over, as though on cue, and placed more curry onto my plate, urging me to take second servings. Looking at him, I shook my head. But when he didn't notice, I raised my hand up slightly in protest, saying "No, no, no."

"You have to eat and become *big*," he said, widening his eyes playfully to emphasize the word. "How else are you going to be a doctor?" Although he was giggling, I knew he was pretty serious. Everyone in my family is pretty serious about me becoming an anesthesiologist, a surgeon or a doctor at the least . . . everyone except me.

Behind the unceasing smile and the sweet words, my father is aged, lives a colorless life, and is strained in every way due to interminable anxiety. The pain exists but is always hidden. He may not know, but just a glance in his direction and I can tell. The only thing remaining on his bucket list is to be able to pay off my college loans and see me a happily graduated doctor—or in any position really, as long as it is a prosperous position in the medical field. This is his "light at the end of the tunnel;" his happiness lies in my successful future. And in short, my happiness lies in his happiness. I half-smiled back at him and continued to chew the rest of the food. With it, I chewed down the desires I had for myself. I chuckled in my head and pushed aside all the hopes I had of becoming an educator, a writer, or a nonprofit entrepreneur. Throughout the rest of dinner, my father spoke about all kinds of things, but I quickly lost interest and found myself drifting away with thoughts of my future.

"Where did I want to be in ten years? Would I even be able to become a doctor? And if by a miracle I did, would I truly be happy?" I questioned myself. After we finished eating, I took on the job of washing the dishes. As I scrubbed grease off of plates and played with lukewarm water, I allowed myself to think of and compare two different lifestyles: one of a doctor and the other of the woman I wanted to be. I already knew the answer, but for the sake of reconsidering, I asked myself again, "Which would make me happier?"

I didn't want to reconsider. I wanted to go with my gut feeling and blindly decide. I wanted to live my life by doing the things I love and feel passionate about. But if I do, my father will be hurt for eternity. He'll never show it or speak of it, but he is my hero, and I know this would break his heart. I am everything he has. I am his dream, his *prize child*. If I don't fulfill his dreams, who will?

As any parent, he has expectations and hopes for me. And who was I to break them like this? *I* would never be happy if I did.

After all, whatever I think my passions are, they aren't nearly as valuable as the passion I have to see my father's smile—one filled with

sincere glee and pride. The day I see this, I will have achieved my
happiness.

BUSHRA MIAH was born in New York, NY. She attended Vanguard High School in
New York, NY, and Long Island University's Arnold and Marie Schwartz College of
Pharmacy in Brooklyn, NY.

A Time for Healing

BY MARLYN PALOMINO, 2011

I have been avoiding this, but I found myself alone today and thought it was the perfect time to *Get It Done*. To cry as much as I can. To let all these buried feelings come out and to say the words and see them on paper. Mom—my first word, and my first loss. My memories of her have shaped me.

I look back and it feels like I'm paralyzed. My mind fights hard to send commands but I can't speak. Fear has sewn my lips together and cut out my tongue. I scream . . . I mumble . . . I purr. I want to rip all my hair out; I want to feel pain. Familiar voices are calling me. What do they want? Am I insane? The voices are getting louder, telling me that my mother has gone to heaven. The voices are the enemy, invisible but strong, squeezing and breaking me apart. I am flying at the speed of light. I can't stop. Is this a game? I'm not playing. I want to disappear.

Am I now the mommy? Fear knows me . . . knows my weakest point, what I'm scared of the most. Growing up, I always had a fear about the day she would be gone. Who would I be left with? My father?

I feel like throwing up right now, but I can still hear my mother's voice, singing by the moon: *Sana que sana colita de rana si no sanas hoy sanarás mañana.* "Heal, heal little tail of the frog. If you don't heal today, you'll heal tomorrow."

When my mother died of cancer in 2008, I lost my way. Everything turned dark because my shining light had shut down. I would wake up every morning and call her name, but it was too late. I wondered if it was my fault. I had no reason to go on, no direction, nothing—just a deadbeat father, a cold-blooded snake—silent, always hiding and stalking his prey, ready to inject his venom to kill a hope. Fear defeated me; it was so mean.

But a force kept pushing me forward, dragging me against my will. It was a strength—a healing power—like the *sanarás* of my mother's song. Now I know that healing revives—it brings a new state but never the original one. Healing recovers and extracts the pain. Healing moves on but never forgets. My mother is gone, but only physically—she will always be alive in my mind and heart. My father was never a father figure. He's a blurry image fading away into ashes. He cannot hurt me now.

My healing feels slow, but I know it is always mending me, making me whole. Scars are still forming, but they give me strength, help me grow physically and mentally, and toughen me so that I am able to take risks, take advantage of opportunities, and use my talents wisely. I am positive. I am resilient. I am a survivor.

MARLYN PALOMINO was born in Miami, FL, and raised in Bogotá, Colombia. She attended Flushing International High School in Flushing, NY and Queen's College in Queens, NY.

The Photograph

BY ALEXA BETANCES, 2016

My mother lies on her hospital bed in the city of Moca in the Dominican
Republic. Weary and worn, she manages to raise her head to look at the
camera, the reflection of the bright ash on the soft, lemon-green colored
walls in the background. There are two beds separated by a little white
table. My mother lies in one bed; my baby bag on the other. On the bed
beside her sits my father, one arm casually on the headboard, the other
arm cradling my baby body.

As I look at this photograph and my father's facial expression while
holding me, I don't see the big scary man who rarely shows emotion usually described in family stories. I see a different man—his tough exterior
gone. While my mother looks at the camera, my father looks down at me,
as if he is trying to grasp every detail of his firstborn. His eyes are so
relaxed—an expression so clear and vivid, still so unreadable.

What thoughts are running through his mind while he gazes down at
me? Is he wondering how my future will look? What my favorite food
would be? My interests, dislikes, friends? Will I prefer to wear skirts or
pants? Heels or sneakers? Will my hair be long or short? All the details
that create the person I am today. Did he know where this picture would
end up—stuffed deep in my drawer with the rest of the blurred

memories he left behind? Did he know he would only be present for three years of my life? Did he know I would be looking at this picture right now—almost sixteen years later, a sophomore in high school—wondering what went wrong? Would you have stopped it, Dad? Wished it away?

Most of my life, you were only a pile of old photographs and sudden, quick phone calls asking how I've been; then, with a nonchalant whisper, I'd say, "Good," knowing it would be different if you were here. The phone calls would have been face-to-face conversations, laughing and checking up on each other. Those old photographs would have been photographs of recent trips we took together—trips to the movies, to the beach, photographs of new experiences and memories being made all the time. They wouldn't be blurry because I was too young to remember them; they would be blurry because there would be too many of them to keep track.

Analyzing this photograph—my father's facial expression and the story behind it—used to be part of my daily routine. But over the years, this burden has turned into an object. A photograph that used to symbolize my father's inner thoughts is now as dull as a brick wall. The tears and empty feeling triggered by this image have turned into an unfamiliar feeling. It's not a careless feeling; instead, it has shaped my mind-set. Something I have no control over should not be forgotten, but it also should not weigh me down. My grandma used to say, "Write it on a small piece of paper; fold it until it's too small to be folded again; hold it in your fist; blow on it, and that's it."

It disappears.

ALEXA BETANCES was born in Moca, Dominican Republic, and grew up in Queens, NY. She attended Urban Assembly School for Law & Justice in Brooklyn, NY.

Still Looking

BY CEASIA KING, 2010

When I first moved, lying in her womb, I thought that she would speak to me. Instead, I heard the loud voices of the people surrounding her. I began to kick so they would realize that "Hello, I'm going to be her last child!" However, what I did not know is that I would end up falling in the middle, the third seed to be released from my mother's womb.

Then, no longer kicking and protected by my mother's skin, I was able to smell her scent. It was like knowing who I was before anyone ever told me who I was going to be. I embraced the moment and since then, I transitioned from an embryo looking for a way out of my mother's womb to a seventeen-year-old looking for a way back in.

Now I sit and wonder, staring up at the ceiling, trying to remember when she's been there for me. I wonder when she decided that I would be the child she wanted to brag about, yet the one she would manage to hurt. In some ways, I thought her bragging about me was her way of showing her strength and her character as a mother. I've come to realize that it's more about her holding on to her pride, not letting anyone see her break down.

I'll never forget when my grandmother passed away. To me, it was as if the world skipped my favorite season and went from fall to spring. To my mother, it was like racing through her favorite season just to leave all the past memories behind. I wondered whether she wanted to deny the fact that her mother was gone because she just couldn't face it or because she didn't know how to face it. She sat there after hearing the news about her mother, and she began to make phone calls. She went from having watery eyes to smiles and laughter. With the look of a daughter only somewhat devastated, she proved to me that she was not an emotional person. I began to think that watery eyes and being strong for the family wasn't the right way to express her devastation. Through it all, I concluded that she didn't quite know how to express her grief for the passing of my grandmother.

I began to wonder why she responds the way she does and why I look so deeply into her decisions. Like when she decided that her boyfriend would reside in our house, or when she decided she would lie and say she was coming back one night when she knew she wasn't coming home for the whole weekend. Or when she's trying to bribe me, saying things like "It would be nice for you to get out of the house for a little while" so she could have company over, or when she doesn't quite know how to ask me simple questions like "How did your meeting go?" Why haven't I just accepted the way she is? Instead I resist and respond in ways that she probably never thought I would. I've said, "Oh, gosh here we go," and "I live here, so I'm not going anywhere, how you gon' try to kick your own children out?" Then walked away, not wanting to feel the pain, and began writing.

Then I wonder, why do I write when I feel this pain? Is it my mother who influences me, by her lack of understanding of my life and my identity? I sit there and write, letting the pen lead me on to the next line. I begin to feel as though my thoughts aren't making any sense. So, I think about how she doesn't realize she's hurting me. I've been through it all with her. From the lies to the laughter, late-night sessions of crying uncontrollably, only to lie on soaked pillows and scream only so no one would hear me. I sat up in the dark and began to write, realizing that my words are what have been saving me day after day. It's because of the struggle of having a true relationship with my mother that I've been able to write some of my strongest poems. When she avoids my feelings of self-consciousness, or my struggle to be comfortable with who I am, when she punches me in my heart without even using her fists but by doing the things she does and saying the things she says, my deepest fears and my truest feelings are revealed through my writing.

I sit around, still looking up at the ceiling, and think about how I ended up the way I am. Am I a reflection of my mother, or are my writings a reflection of my need for her to be there for me?

Either way, I continue to write without thoughts of love and care, instead with thoughts of neglect and shame. As I sit there thinking, remembering, I realize that there is no reason for me to remain seated, so I begin to look away from my mother's eyes and stand on my own.

CEASIA KING was born in Brooklyn, NY. She attended Millennium High School in New York, NY, and Syracuse University in Syracuse, NY.

Work

BY SHANNON DANIELS, 2014

The August air hung, like overripe fruit, over my body until we got the car going. I leaned out the window, and my hair came alive with grease and wind. We beat back miles of New York highway. Dea sang and Andrew cracked jokes. Our laughter condensed like raindrops on the windshield. We let the songs on the radio stream out the windows. We giggled and groaned and leaned back in our seats. We talked about love like it'd just dropped by for a chat one morning—what we had done, how many edges and corners had we seen, every smell, every taste, as if they were things we could keep in jars to hang on a shelf. We wasted summer days on yellow-and-white lines—hours away from the beaded sarongs and sweet, sweet fudge of Long Beach Island, yet miles away from the carpeted office floors and water coolers of New York—but we wouldn't have had it any other way.

Days like these were a respite from my first summer job: lifting elbow after elbow of rope over a boat's railing, waiting for rusted cages and twine nets to materialize out of the Hudson. On particularly hot and slow days, I reasoned that in some other universe I was captain of the *Lilac*. Instead of fending off blue crabs, the interns and I battled enemy crews. We weren't pulling up nets for population studies but probing for buried treasure. And on the ship, I would stay a lanky fifteen-year-old girl forever—that part took the most believing.

What I did believe, without a doubt, was that time took a break from its job to burn change at the arcade with us at Long Beach Island, lick powdered sugar off its oily fingers, and tuck seashell bits into our pockets. The stores, the restaurants, the fudge flavors, the sunshine—these were as immobile as any sidewalk or shore. Andrew, Dea, and I had never seen a sunset on the island—even now, it's preserved irrevocably this way in my mind, like summer raspberries that still taste good in November. We ate our fudge on the same bench every time. We'd talk about music videos and pranks and groan about summer assignments—"not again." Then we'd search, like a scholar for rare documents, for some idea of who we wanted to be five, ten, twenty years from now. Would we still like Billy Joel and sing "My Heart Will Go On" over and over until we got the notes just right? Would we live on opposite ends of the globe? Would we still pretend life hadn't begun so that we could imagine the champagne flutes, reworks, and contained laughter of adulthood for hours on end?

I thought about work—my work. What I pushed up the hill every day of that summer wasn't a rock like Sisyphus but buckets of seawater. So many people told me that I should get used to work, *real* work like this: day in, day out. A schedule, a to-do list, and bosses. This is what I have been doing ever since. The offices are different and the carpeting under my feet changes every year, but I am becoming slowly, irreversibly "mature." I have sacrificed beach days and swing sets and laughter-filled afternoons. I've rethought my wardrobe, attended interviews, and explained in more essays than I can imagine who I am. I have worked hard—but this is only half of it.

The most laborious tasks cannot be spell-checked by Word or alphabetized by Excel. The real work is this—*this* right here. Resurrecting the long-gone—conversations my trio of friends had, dismissed, and brought up again and again. Remembering the taste of air in New York City during one exact summer, on one exact day. Remembering the people

I've met and the smells of their homes, the boys who kissed me and the ones who spurned me, the texture of uncertainty in all of its crevices. Recording it all abashedly, unashamedly. Bringing the dead back to life —and bringing life back to life. This is an endless, ravenous duty that I love. This is real work: pulling armfuls of rope out of the water and seeing what treasures live in its murky depths.

SHANNON DANIELS was born in New York, NY. She attended Stuyvesant High School in New York, NY, and Stanford University in Stanford, CA.

Noriko's Postcards

BY MONA HADDAD, 2009

Noriko came to visit every few months or so, every time she took a break
from her travels. She sent me postcards from all of her trips, and I'd col-
lect them in her absence, tracking her trek across the globe from Eighty-
Sixth Street, learning of Holland, of Japan, of Los Angeles. She came to
see my mother, but I like to think she stayed for me. Every time she
visited, she would play with me, going along with whatever my interests
were at the time.

Once, we had a Bugs Bunny wedding. I was the bride, my giant Bugs
Bunny stuffed animal was the groom, and she was the flower girl, the
facilitator, and the guests, all at once. I couldn't find flowers, so we threw
Band-Aids left and right as we marched down the aisle, setting the scene
for my big day. We sang the Japanese children's songs she had taught me,
and by the end of the afternoon, Bugs Bunny, who was dressed in the
tuxedo he came with, went from the star of the wedding (second to me,
of course) to a wallflower, as Noriko and I danced to my mother's records
and ate Oreos at the reception.

Not long after, Noriko left again to travel and did not return for years.
I continued to receive postcards, but as time went on, the intervals
between them grew further and further apart. Her last postcard came

almost a decade after Bugs Bunny's wedding. She had written to tell me how she had decided to marry a real groom and to stay in Los Angeles for good. She attached pictures of her "children," two plush kittens named Jim and Aaron, and asked how my marriage was going. By then, Bugs Bunny no longer fit in my life or my room, which was covered with books and preteen possessions, and was boxed up and sent to storage.

Soon after, through a conversation with my mother, I learned that Noriko traveled, not only to explore, but also to escape. Born the daughter of a Japanese princess, she renounced her title upon rejecting her arranged marriage. She traveled the world to find a new home, I imagine, and sent me that last postcard when she finally found it, to let me know that she was okay and that everything that wasn't would soon be, too.

MONA HADDAD was born in New York, NY. She attended Hackley School in Tarrytown, NY, and Mount Holyoke College in South Hadley, MA.

The Rebirth of Shanai Williams

SHANAI WILLIAMS, 2017

Home of seven to a house of two
Once a place of love and joy
They've all moved on and left you

My head was dizzy with anticipation as I approached the blue double doors. It was my first day of freshman year, and I stared at my high school with so much hope. A sense of independence washed over me as well as an undeniable determination to succeed where I had failed before. This was my chance. I longed for a herd of people to call my own. I ascended the steps sure that I'd find at least one person, the person who I'd imagined would click together with me like Lego pieces.

The previous four years had been riddled with the loss of myself. My parents had split, which meant my brother and sisters did too. I was no longer the happy kid in a home of seven. The people who had given me my original sense of where I belonged in the world slowly went their separate ways. I craved the guidance and security I suddenly lacked. What better place to look than a high school full of hormonal teenagers?

When I entered homeroom, my smile bright, teeth reflecting all my ambitions in life, I was met with quiet, blank stares from the white faces staring back. My smile dissolved as I took the nearest seat. I attempted small talk with the three people at my shared table to no avail. I was ignored. I got the message and kept to myself.

> *But at this*
> *Intersection?*
> *of being a Black, Bisexual, Girl*
> *I am unsure?*
> *Where?*
> *to Rise.*

The wrinkled nose, the scrunched-up face. Here we go again. *"What's 'chopped' mean?"* I'd made friends, but I couldn't carry a conversation without having to explain the slang I was using. I longed for my Bronx peers. The boisterous, confident, care-free mix of black and Hispanic kids. The kids that understood me and kept me laughing, the ones who made me feel at home. Without them I was lost.

"Stop crying!" my mother yelled at me.

How? I couldn't understand how she could possibly think it was that easy. I wasn't angry at her for leaving without putting up a fight. I wasn't angry at my father for making her go. It was the slow progression of the only home I've ever known being broken apart that hurt. My father barely picked up my younger sister anymore, and visits from my older sisters became rare. My older brother moved entirely, not seeing any reason to stay since our mom left. My daddy's job consumed his time but for his two hobbies: sleep and hunting for women. I was shoved into a house full of strangers. And she wanted me to "stop crying."

> *Where?*
> *Do I fit?*
> *Where is?*

My opening?
Must I create it for
Myself?

"You're too nice," my close friend told me, after telling her about another ex who had taken advantage of me. I agreed, but I didn't see how that was really possible.

Isn't being nice a part of being a good person? Aren't I a good a person? So why don't people stay? Is this what I deserve?

"*Uni* meaning one. *Verse* meaning song, you have a part to play in this song so grab that microphone and be brave, sing your heart out on life's stage. You cannot go back and make a brand-new beginning. But you can start now and make a brand new . . . ending." There, in the words of Prince Ea's motivational video I'd almost passed scrolling through Facebook, I had found the Lego piece I needed. Something clicked in me that night and the tears would not stop falling. My family would never reunite in a single household again. No matter how much my friends tried they would never be able to provide me with the security I sought. My joy wasn't anyone else's responsibility. But just because no one else could give me the things I sought, that didn't mean that I couldn't have them. I still had Myself.

I decided then I would no longer be imprisoned by the impulse to find an easy solution so that I can return to life as usual. I will no longer look to other people to fill the voids in my life. I will no longer base my worth on how other people treat me.

I may never have all the answers and I know I'm going to make mistakes. My pain won't completely dissipate, but it will subside as long as I am actively striving to better myself. I will experience disappointment and pain but I will get through it, because that's how life is. Good times will come, along with the right people who will treat me the way I deserve, because I know better than to allow anyone to give me any less.

Home of seven to a home of one
This isn't what you expected?
But it's a just platform?
To use the knowledge you've collected.

SHANAI WILLIAMS was born in New York, NY. She attended NYC iSchool and The King's College in New York, NY.

"And this is what stories do: they let us know that no matter how different and unique we are and how isolated we may feel, someone else has been there, someone else has survived, and someone else has made it out. Telling our stories is a revolutionary act."

--JANET MOCK--

Monolid Monologue

BY BECKY CHAO, 2011

Mommie says that I'm very *lang lui*. *Beautiful girl*. I don't believe it. If she really thought I was beautiful, she wouldn't be constantly bemoaning my monolids. But you may not know what a monolid is. I didn't either, until a few years ago. Microsoft Word doesn't even think that "monolid" is a word. You type it in, and you get that angry, jagged red scribble. When you spell-check, the software suggests that maybe you meant "moonlit," or "monolith," or "moonblind"—is *moonblind* even a word?

A quick Google search will tell you that a monolid is "an eyelid without a crease, common to many ethnic Asians"—like me!

Ever since I was little, my mother has gone on and on about how she has no clue where my eyelids came from.

"Everybody in the family has that eyelid fold," she says. "I don't understand where yours went!"

Um. Yeah, Mom, sorry my eyelid fold decided to walk itself on my face. I don't know, maybe it just thought I should look even more like an "ethnic Asian."

It's a bit ironic, since I'm definitely not the most enthusiastic Asian out there. I'm not big on Chinese culture at all. I don't know any of those boy bands who all look and sound the same, like Super Junior? Fahrenheit? Say what?

I can't even speak the language. It's a little sad. My Cantonese is all over the place. I mispronounce syllables. My pitch is all wrong. And don't even get me started on those idioms.

All those holidays? Mooncake day? I don't even know the meaning behind it—I just like the mooncakes.

So why am I the one stuck with the monolids, here?

Over the years, my mother never made me feel any better about it. Somehow, she worked the subject of my monolids into every phone call, family dinner, and reunion. It became something that we joked about: "Oh, haha, Becky's weird—she's got a monolid that came from who knows where!"

But I like to entertain the fantasy that maybe I got mixed up at birth. It makes sense! 'Cause, you know, monolids are all in the genetics. And monolids are nowhere else to be found in the Chao family. There was a time in eighth grade when Danny, this kid in my class, called me out on being a fake Chinese. I was "too white" to be Chinese, he said. I had to be Japanese! That would explain my short fling with anime in the summer after sixth grade. I was crazy about it: Black Cat, Inuyasha—I watched almost all of them. And it would explain why I suck so much at speaking Chinese—because I'm not meant to speak it! Okay, so maybe I'm exaggerating a little. To be honest, I suck at *all* languages. English, Becky?

Man, do you even *listen* to yourself? But it doesn't really matter if I'm Japanese or Chinese, because I'm still gonna have my monolids. And the truth is, at this point, I've learned to take my mom's jokes about my monolids in stride.

She says that I'm very *lang lui*.

Beautiful girl.

I guess I should be fine with that.

BECKY CHAO was born in New York, NY. She attended Stuyvesant High School in New York, NY, and Duke University in Durham, NC.

This Is My Dwelling

BY AMANDA DAY McCULLOUGH, 2012

Repetition numbs. Or at least it's supposed to. But watching the foliage of upstate New York flash past the window of my dad's battle-worn Toyota, I remember the countless times its tires jostled me over the bumps and potholes of the parkway. It's the road that always transports me from the blinding lights and blaring horns of Queens Boulevard to that pale blue house mounted atop the steepest hill in Westchester. The road that was once met with a chorus of *are we there yets* is now given the silent treatment.

I will never know the exact moment when the car ride changed for me. Probably because there isn't an exact moment. I like exact moments. They make things clearer in my mind, a sort of timeline of myself. As kids, my sister Meghan and I raced to the car. We itched to get to the blue house and play with our cousins, Dan and Lizzie. But I take my time today, dragging my feet. When I climb in the car my heart constricts. The Toyota reeks of the soured expectations of past rides.

My parents, Meghan, and I haven't seen my Aunt Jess, Dan, or Lizzie since last Christmas.

"Will Dan be there?" I ask, my voice cracking. I know he avoids that house like it's rotting, even when I'm there. But I have to ask anyway.

"Maybe. That shouldn't matter, though," my mom replies.

I sigh. Of course it matters. Whether it SHOULD or not . . . I can't say. I know by my sister's eye rolling that she thinks I'm stupid for caring. She got over our family a long time ago.

The first and only time Meghan and I slept over at the blue house I was ten and she was thirteen. That night, before the classic, Westchesterian "I-can't-see-my-hand-waving-in-front-of-my-face" darkness set in, all four of us cousins jammed our way onto the narrow wooden swing behind the blue house. It was tethered to a stubby branch with yellow rope. Lizzie's bony hip jutted into my side while Dan's preteen body laid horizontally across the three of us, the swing spinning so fast that the blue house blurred into the sapphire sky behind it. We shrieked and squealed and yelled. It was about thirty seconds before we all fell backwards to the ground. The swing danced around the tree in the absence of our weight, laughing at us. But we were laughing, too. I laughed hardest when I discovered I'd cut my knee on the tree's roots. At the time, the cut solidified our fun, fun that, in the end, was as wispy as the swing's thinning, yellow rope.

The thing about being a kid is that when you experience something really amazing, something out-of-this-world fantastic, it becomes your standard for measuring all other experiences. In that way, you literally set yourself up for disappointment. Everything changes, and you're still hanging on to that memory. For years I bothered my cousins about getting back on the swing, but we never did. Today, going to the blue house is still about seeing Dan and Lizzie, but it's a Dan whose ear is pierced and a Lizzie whose eyeliner is darker than the onyx night of the sleepover.

At subsequent visits to the blue house, whenever voices were raised, or doors slammed, I would escape the house and swing for a while. The swing was the one remnant of the sleepover, proof that the day had actually existed in the first place. But it could never support the weight of four kids now. The swing was splintering and crooked, the rope frayed. Was it the aftermath of that one adventure? Or maybe it had always been brittle and I just hadn't noticed.

We zoom past a car with a dented bumper and broken headlights. I think about all the brokenness of the blue house. There is the house itself, and then there are the people living in it, who seem to be broken, too. And there are the memories, of course, which are themselves intact but break the people who dwell incessantly on the past. People like me. As we park our car on the hill, this is what I'm thinking about. How things are broken, and how they can't always be fixed. Because by glorifying one moment among hundreds, by trying to bring the house back to a less broken time, I started to break myself. And I don't want to be just another broken thing in the pale blue house.

We wait a few moments before getting out of the car. My sister's face is emotionless: it's just a routine. I push open the door, and glance toward the tree near the back of the house. The stubby branch has been severed. The swing is gone.

AMANDA DAY McCULLOUGH was born in New York, NY. She attended Hunter College High School in New York, NY, and Pomona College in Claremont, CA.

Where I'm From

BY SAMANTHA WHITE, 2008

I'm from the place of *oodles*. The place of Skelly courts and handball. Basketball sounds is my alarm clock. The police is the snooze button. RnB, rap, reggae, and soca dress me in the morning. Manhattan skylines are out my window. Close, as if I can touch them in the morning as the sun rises over the buildings.

Walk into the kitchen I see walls that reflect every house in the building. I smell bacon emerging from the microwave as I look into the home of Kool-Aid. I enter the living room of generations to blast the same song that echoes through everyone's ears in every house. I walk back into my kitchen and look back in my fridge as if hoping to see something new.

I leave my house and get in the elevator with each floor being a different smell. Fried chicken, curry, ribs, fish, macaroni and cheese . . . so many. Step out a broken metal door with a magnet that don't work. See the area that looks like a mini family reunion. Little kids running around. Parents yelling to get their point across. Older kids running; police following. Onlookers being nosy. See the same group of people that you hang out with every so often.

It's nighttime and you feel the wind picking up. You watch those sexy figures pushing and shoving, playing basketball. Well, some sexy and some you just wonder why. Can't help it.

You feel the vibrations in the air from all the moving on the ground. You hear echoes of a fight breaking out. Already expecting to hear rings in your ear. Just move to the next basketball court or sneak in and out of the fight area. Whichever happens you still get a good show. Meet up with your friends, hang out some more. Get tired, split your ways and go into the house. The window becomes your eyes and ears to the live hood. Whatever happens, happens, and you go to sleep to wake up and do it again.

SAMANTHA WHITE was born in Brooklyn, NY. She attended Urban Assembly School for Music and Art and Kingsborough Community College in Brooklyn, NY, and Hunter College in New York, NY.

My Vietnam

BY SASHA GOODFRIEND, 2009

When I used to think of Vietnam, I would think of teenagers with flowers in their hair and leather miniskirts, arm in arm with boys in bell-bottoms and fists in the air, marching against the Vietnam War. I would start humming "Aquarius" and sigh at the idea of "our young men" dying in war. Last summer I was fortunate enough to go backpacking with my mom and explore the real Vietnam.

Now when I think of Vietnam I think of the smile that spreads across my face when I successfully bring spring rolls to my mouth using chopsticks. I feel my backpack thumping on my back as I trekked in the hilltribes in the Hòa Bình province. My fingers twitch, wishing to peel away, the bright pink curls of dragon-fruit skin and slurp the white fruits insides. I look to see a faded billboard of wartime propaganda in the distance, muffled by swarms of conical hats.

I still tense up at the idea of crossing the street, dense with motorcycles, some with families of five piled on nonchalantly, while other motorcycles sport office women in heels. It wasn't uncommon to see a man with a basket full of pigs strapped onto the back of his bike, or another's overflowing with woven baskets.

When I walk out of my house in the early morning, sleep still in my eyes, I can faintly smell fresh fish from the market. I search for teetering steps in front of me, shadowed by the baskets balanced on a wooden beam on a tired shoulder to show me the way. I can see the golden yellow robes of a pair of Buddhist monks huddled together out of the corner of my eye. I can squat for hours in the same position, leaning on the backs of my heels.

When I am startled by the loud sounds of garbage trucks, I am reminded of the loudest sound I've ever heard, the booming of the M16s from the Cuchi Tunnels. In the morning trying to remember where I am, while swiping my MetroCard on the way to school, between bites at lunch, and while gazing out the window in math class, these are the images and senses that flood my head. This is how I remember Vietnam.

SASHA GOODFRIEND grew up in Manhattan, NY. She attended NYC Lab School for Collaborative Studies in New York, NY, and Boston University and Simmons College in Boston, MA.

On Thermodynamics: A Reflection

BY EN YU ZHANG, 2017

Second law of thermodynamics: the entropy of an isolated system always increases

$\therefore$ *Energy must be added to maintain the integrity of the system*

Since an isolated system must constantly have an input of energy so as to not fall into disorder, then that system is not truly isolated; the energy must come from another source. However, the idea of a truly isolated system is a beautiful idea. The mind, the consciousness, is the epitome of such a system, contained within one person, seemingly impenetrable but so easily molded by the outside world. And just as the mind is influenced by reality, the perspective of reality is shaped by the mind.

As such, a reclusive person like myself has a more closed-off worldview. At home, I keep myself within as much as possible. Staying connected to that place allows my mind the liberty of not straying beyond my vision of a comfortable world. It is not that I find the outside world to be frightening and stress-inducing with the challenges of human interaction; I simply am satisfied with such a "low" standard. There was nothing wrong with the hours of solitude I went through every day, nothing wrong with the monotony.

I knew exactly what activities I could do in that room: distract myself with the computer, read a book, take a nap, or do homework. Of course, the last option was only there to trick my mind into thinking that I was on the verge of productivity at any moment. I kept my world under strict control, repeating these activities in orders of my choosing, needing not to think long and hard about anything. As such, I lived in a tranquil, comforting world, just doing whatever I wished, without concerns about future repercussions. Inside my head full of illusions, I thought that I had already fulfilled what I needed to do each day.

The realization came slowly to me, through seeing my peers climb their way up, achieving beyond what I barely even thought necessary. There was the girl, after last year's annual math competition, who studied intensively for this year's, in contrast to myself, who was only reminded of its existence a month before the test, and then still did nothing. There was the girl doubling up in PreCal and Calculus while being a track star. There was the math-team genius who scored a perfect 150 on the math competition. There was the classmate whose eloquence in class I could never hope to emulate. As I directed my eyes beyond my bubble, to expand beyond myself, I saw myself as nothing. I was nothing, just empty space in comparison, whittling my time away in comfort induced by blindness. An isolated system would yield nothing of the sort that they reached.

My isolated system could not be maintained at this point. My sleeping habits were jumbled up, my homework done half-heartedly, my grades great but nothing all too stellar. Everything was becoming disordered, tearing apart at the seams.

Free energy $= \Delta G = \Delta H - T\Delta S$

$\Delta H = $ *change in enthalpy*

T = *temperature*

ΔS = *change in entropy*

A reaction is spontaneous, that is, occurs when ΔG > 0.

∴ Spontaneity is favored by an increase in entropy and a decrease in enthalpy.

This begs the fundamental question of whether or not I was able to take action. I tried, perhaps bearing the best of intentions, but not the most unbending will. I would have a somewhat productive day, only to spoil it at the end by falling asleep hours too early. Sometimes it was waking up early on a weekend morning to complete one assignment, only to then succumb to the computer and be released of the trance in the evening.

I am spurred to action when everything undoes itself even further, becomes even more disorderly, and when there seems to be less work. As such, spontaneity is reached, and I get to work. Reverse psychology acts at its nest here; I become increasingly more motivated if the world pushes against me, as if to prove to it that I can do what is seemingly impossible for me.

Then, other days, when I seem to have more of my world under control, perhaps after a productive yesterday, the days I have difficult assignments I want to avoid, then I regress; there is no spontaneity then. There is no change. Such is the continuation of the cycle.

EN YU ZHANG was born in Hong Kong. She attended Stuyvesant High School in New York, NY.

Life in Senegal

BY YVONNE NDIAYE, 2010

I still remember the smell of the house, the neighborhood, and the city. The house is shaped like a quarter; my room is inside but the windows are outside. The lack of freedom: always hear her saying, "You better be home at 5:30 PM or you won't get your lunch." I never answer. I always look up and down and walk away.

I can hear my grandfather cursing at me because I wasn't born in a marriage. I can see the faces of jealousy because I go to a private school and I wear decent clothes—everyone admires me. I can see the love and the hate fighting with each other, but I tolerate it and know one day I'll be free.

I can remember the look of happiness on their faces because I don't go to school anymore and I can cook for them. I remember the death of my cousin, brother, grandmother, and an uncle I didn't know in 1999. I lived in Senegal for ten years.

YVONNE NDIAYE was born in the Bronx, NY, and grew up in Senegal and New York, NY. She attended Brooklyn International High School in Brooklyn, NY, and Onondaga Community College in Syracuse, NY.

Autism Is...

BY CHARLENE VASQUEZ, 2015

Autism. This word can mean anything to anyone. It's such a varied term; those who have it can't express what it is either. It is not something you can feel—or touch. Autism? Oh no, it is much more than that. Autism is color; it is complexity. It is day and night, happy and sad. It's not one thing only, and it is not rare. Although this is my own opinion that I speak, autism can be anything. There is no definite answer as to what it is or what it is not. Merely, autism is.

It never occurred to me that autism affected my whole life—oh, but I was wrong. I was diagnosed at birth, and it startled my mother. Was I sick? It was such a foreign conception. I was the first child to be diagnosed in my family of three siblings, and so she cried. Tears were shed. It was heartbreaking. My mother, a warrior who ambled on burning coal since her teenage years, had no idea what autism was or if her second daughter would be . . . "mentally ill." With the help of a psychologist, she sought and got help, and she learned along the way that autism can't be "cured." She continued, biting back tears and frustration, to get me to be the very best I could be. It was working, and I, at the age of two, finally learned how to speak. "Mama! Papa!" and it was a mother's miracle. All I could say, she said, were those two words . . . until I stopped altogether by five years old. When I couldn't speak anymore it raised concern. Most of my family members were alerted. Surely it was a mystery.

My mom brought me to the psychologist again for answers to this dilemma and the answer was given—I really did have autism. Imagine this: a friend comes up to you and tells you to get something for them, but you have no idea why they need it but you do it anyway. My mom felt this way about my autism, but she never gave up on trying to get me the right support. Support, huh? I didn't know what that was until I turned ten, and even then I didn't pay any mind to it. My comprehension matched the level of my general age group or higher—so why should I have paid any mind? It wasn't until my mother explained her journey to keep me stable that I was aware of such a word; but that was only the exposure. I still couldn't actually comprehend what that incredibly complex thing was.

Coming of age, that's when I started to open my mind a little more. I fell into a depression at the age of fifteen out of the yearning to not fail in school. Keep in mind that I had support—had. There was a battle between my preference of not wanting to travel to my appointments and the necessity for the appointments, so this caused my mom to shut down my support for about two years. This was happening around the same time that I was transitioning from the private schooling system to public, so my mom had to put a lot of thought into these decisions, which raised questions, too. Was it a mistake to remove my support? Was it a mistake to put me into mainstream after nine years of attending one private school? I was finally placed in public school, with a delicate yet intelligent mind, at thirteen. I prospered like it was a dream that I could vividly see in my sleep. And yet this transition raised another dilemma for me. They put me in sixth grade to begin middle school and once my school guidance teacher noticed something was off, it was eighth grade for me in one year. What a transition!

Now let's fast forward to now. One year in middle school and now I'm in ninth grade. It's not a rare case to skip grades, of course, so I don't have the heart to say it's something I can brag about. Now I roam high school premises wondering who I am and why I do what I do. Bingo, I fell into a pit of darkness and anxiety. Of course, I know everyone gets depressed or anxious, for they would be inhuman if that wasn't the case, but because of this great fall, I realized how capable I am for someone diagnosed with autism and struggling. It surely is evident in my schoolwork, and my principal came up to my mom herself and brought up how remarkable my effort is. Now I wonder, how did I accomplish this? Although, without a doubt, I am capable.

With this capability that I possess, I do notice why I went through what I did. It wasn't easy to distinguish my intelligence and my mental state. Even to my current days, if I am to tell someone that I have this disability, they wouldn't believe me. I don't blame them. It is stereotyped that autistic kids are "incapable." Even I, myself, forget. It's something to focus on but to not fuss over. So, once it leaves your mind, then what? People forget autism, then they forget that autism is a world of differences—no two are the same and we can only acknowledge similarities. Sounds familiar, right? It should sound like the human population; something so diverse that if an alien asks about who and what we are, we would all have different answers. Science has that answer, maybe? But no, humans are not just one thing: we are many things and that applies to autistic children as well. Generalization is easy but not right. Autism isn't one thing; it's many things and it's beautiful, so that should never bring anyone down to hear, "your child has autism."
Autism simply . . . Is.

CHARLENE VASQUEZ was born in New York, NY. She attended Bronx Career & College Preparatory High School and Hostos Community College in Bronx, NY.

Requiem

BY TONI BRUNO, 2007

On the last Christmas that my aunt was alive we played music. We
always play music, but this time we played with a new level of ferocity
and passion. My father hit every piano key as though it was the only
sound worth creating in the world, and cousin Will beat his hands on
the bongos as though he were sacrificing his fingers for his mother's life.
Even my uncle, who was tone deaf and preferred to listen, had joined in,
and the younger cousins whacked tambourines off beat. We had been
playing for hours, and our faces were red. It was a cold December day,
but we were sweating through our T-shirts.

She sat on the couch between her mother and sister, thin and white as
a sheet of paper. Her cheeks were hollowed out as though they'd been
punched in and got stuck that way. She had a scarf wrapped around her
bald head, but it was coming undone and it took too much strength for
her to reach up and fix it, so the loose ends hung down her back. She had
given up wigs a few months before. Wigs were for pretending that everything was okay, and we couldn't pretend anymore. One too many discussions about the future without Aunt Heidi had stripped us of the illusions
created by smiles and wigs. We had been pushed to honesty. Forced to
have raw and heart-breaking conversations we never imagined having,

ones that left us stumbling, shell shocked on the sidewalk outside her house. Ones that left us bolting upright every time the phone rang, our hearts stopping for a second before we answered. But it was Christmas and she was still with us, her closeness to death somehow bringing new energy into the warm room. Energy that infiltrated our music, bringing notes to life and making melodies into dedications.

We played songs from my childhood, ones that my father had sung to me as I was falling asleep so they wove into my dreams and wrote themselves on the inside of my mind. Familiar lyrics took on a new quality on this day, seeming to be filled with messages I had never heard before and simple chords that struck me as unimaginably beautiful. I thought of the way these songs comforted me, the way the gentle guitar accompaniment made me feel safe, and I wondered if after this day they would make me sad.

My aunt sat on the couch and listened, her head tipped back slightly, and we knew that if she were strong enough she would have been smiling. She seemed to know that the music was for her, that we were playing her favorite songs because we were saying goodbye. Once she started singing along, so softly it was almost a whisper, but we heard it as though it were the only sound in the room. As though she were screaming in our ears.

My other aunt stood next to me, and tears ran silently down her cheeks as she sang. Tears that we had kept hidden at past family gatherings. Tears that we held back until we left the room, went for a walk, locked ourselves in the bathroom during Thanksgiving dinner and flushed the toilet to muffle our sobs. Tears that came when we watched movies about death and made us feel ashamed because we didn't want to act like she was already dead.

Those were the wig days. Now they were tears we no longer bothered to hide, because we all knew in our hearts it was the last time.

So, we just kept playing.

As though if we strummed a little harder she would live a little longer. As though if we sang a little louder, she could fight a little harder. As though when we stopped, she too would stop, and we couldn't let that happen. Or maybe we just didn't know what else to do. Maybe we had realized that we couldn't save her, that cancer had somehow beat love. So, we turned to music and hoped that it would be stronger than us. We sang songs from her childhood, songs of resistance and revolution. Music has always been our resistance. We find notes to say "goodbye." Notes to say, "I love you more than I have words to express." Notes to say, "it's okay. You can go. We won't stop playing when you're gone."

TONI BRUNO lives in Brooklyn, NY. She attended LaGuardia Arts High School in New York, NY, and Binghamton University in Binghamton, NY.

Forgiveness, Not Burden

BY JISELLE ABRAHAM, 2017

Driving with my father was always a roller coaster. He was reckless and would often close his eyes and pretend that he was falling asleep on the highway. Sometimes he was for real.

But he always knew how to put a smile on my face—until it was time to go home. I would cry and pout because there was a fear harvested deep inside me, telling me I wouldn't see him again.

And then it happened. I didn't see him again for another year and my tears never stopped falling because of the thought that something bad could happen to him and I would never know.

During his absence, I thought of him a lot. I asked my mom questions like, "Why aren't you and Daddy together anymore?" She would never tell me.

But my older sister had no trouble with giving it to me straight.

"Your father beat Mom badly." Hearing those words ripped my heart right out of my chest.

How could this wonderful man that I love so much do such a thing? Domestic violence was something I only heard or saw on television—it wouldn't happen in my house.

While he was gone, I developed. My mind grew but so did my heart.

I reconnected with him again when I was twelve or thirteen. We were sitting in the truck he drove for work and I knew—now was the time to confront him. We had a good laugh, and then we got on a more serious note about the past. He looked me in my eyes and told me that he would never hit my mother.

He lied to my face.

My mother made sure that I grew up knowing how much my father loved me and that he would never do anything to hurt me. As much as she went through, she never doubted that he was a good father. He was a great one. I knew that, and she knew that, and to her that's all that mattered. The past didn't faze her and she didn't hate him. She had conversations with him as if it never even happened, and I envied that. She'd forgiven him because that's all she could do, and so I followed in her steps.

JISELLE ABRAHAM was born in Brooklyn, NY. She attended Edward R. Murrow High School in Brooklyn, NY, and SUNY Buffalo in Buffalo, NY.

All Over Again

BY SHIRLEYKA HECTOR, 2014

The day before my departure was my mom's birthday. Moving to the United States had been a really tough journey all along the route. Coming here was very difficult, because I had to leave behind the ones I loved and had been attached to for the first thirteen years of my life to come live with a new part of my family.

After being the only child of my mother for twelve years, she became pregnant and gave birth to my baby brother two months after the earthquake hit Haiti in 2010. I started to bond with him so well, but I had to travel and come here in November of that same year.

The afternoon before I left, my mom's forehead was creased all day long, signaling her unhappiness. Her brows were furrowed, breaking my heart even more. By the look on her face, I could tell that that was her saddest birthday. She was making something for my brother and my little cousin; in the meantime, I left to go say my final goodbyes to my close friends who lived a little far from my home. I tried not to cry when I embraced my friends because I was feeling so sad. I had built such great bonds with all of my friends and, because of the earthquake, everything I'd done had started to fall apart. Even though none of us dared to say that our relationships were not going to be the same, we all knew it by the way we hugged each other. I'd known my friend Jenny since we were little kids. We buried our heads in one another's shoulders. Our eyes were filled with tears and our countenances were very downcast and hopeless. I said my tearful goodbyes as quickly as possible and went straight back home because I wanted to spend my last hours, minutes, and seconds with my family.

Back at the house, my youngest and coolest aunt, Eleanor, pulled me aside and told me that the minute I stepped out of the door, my mom had burst out in tears. Aunt Eleanor told me that it was dreadful while she tried to hold back her own tears. "Alright boo! I'll try to calm her down." I replied as I headed for the living room, where I found her sitting with a handkerchief in her hands, crying.

I spoke to her, trying to calm her down, but I ended up crying too. We were crying and hugging each other like we would never see each other ever again in the future. Now that we were going to be apart, the time seemed to fly by so fast. I felt drained. I had never felt that emptiness ever in my life before. I did not know what to think of. I did not know what to do. I did not know what to say to soothe the both of us, because we needed comfort correspondingly. We needed it so bad, I swear.

I went to bed with a terrible headache and a sticky face. My mom came and sat beside me on the bed quietly. She did not say anything, not even a word, so I just laid face down on my pillow. I was knocked out after a few minutes.

I woke up in the middle of the night to the sobbing sound of my mother next to me. "You haven't gotten any sleep at all!" I exclaimed. "I have a headache," she said, answering my hidden question. "I feel like my head is being split by a machete." From that moment on, everything my mom said just broke my heart more and more. I felt hopeless for once because my mom was suffering and I was not able to do anything about it. Whenever I looked at her, I felt like someone was pulling my heart out of my chest. I became paralyzed from internal pain for a moment.

I rose up from my sleeping position to caress her pretty, long jet-black hair. I made her lay her head on me to comfort her a little. I looked over to my brother's crib and found out that he wasn't there. My aunt always liked to take him into her room at night, so I knew he was with her. I was a very protective sister to him. Aunt Eleanor just had that passion for taking care of little babies.

The next morning we got ready to go to the airport. I went to say bye to my grandma, aunties, and cousins. It was so heartbreaking. I felt like my life was being torn apart, but I had to go. The moment had finally arrived for me to depart.

My mom and I got into the car that picked us up to go to the airport. When we arrived at the airport, at the entrance, we embraced each other. She said, "I will always adore you, my baby!" I looked deep into her eyes and replied, "I know, Mom! I will love you for infinity!" She kissed me on my forehead and I kissed her back on her cheek. She managed to give me a smile anyway, despite her sadness. I smiled back, trying to restrain the tears forming in my eyes. I gave her a huge hug, telling her that I'd call her as soon as I landed. I patted her back while she did the same to me.

Then I walked away rapidly, giving her my back as quickly as possible so she wouldn't see the tears running down my cheeks. When I got to my gate, all I did was cry, recalling childhood memories with her. I remembered us talking about relationships under a tree in Jacmel, where our family is from. I remembered us running in the rain along the country-side, laughing like two best friends. I remembered her teaching me how to cook in the kitchen. I remembered us eating ice cream on the beach and joking around. (I felt terrible leaving Haiti and my headache came back. It hurt more than before.) I had to leave my homeland because my dad wanted me to come live with him. He had left Haiti when I was only four, leaving me alone with my mother. This was an opportunity for him to get to know me better.

An hour later the airplane came and I got on board. I slept during the whole trip. I only woke up to go use the bathroom.

Four hours later, I finally woke up when the plane was landing. The view of New York from the plane was magnificent. Lights were shining everywhere and the sea bordered the land so delightfully. That's when I first saw the city that never sleeps. I was so amazed by the view. That was the best memory of my journey. I saw the city in which I would be starting my new life, for the worst or the better. New York would be my new home, my new territory to pursue my dreams and build a future.

SHIRLEYKA HECTOR was born in Port-au-Prince, Haiti. She attended International High School at Lafayette in Brooklyn, NY, and Skidmore College in Saratoga Springs, NY.

The Sky's the Limit

BY RAYHANA MAAROUF, 2013

Airplanes have captivated me from a very young age. My friends loved playing with Barbie and Ken dolls, but nothing delighted me more as a kid than taking daily walks with my father past Aviation High School in the neighborhood where my family lived—Sunnyside, Queens. At the time, I was unaware that the students who studied there learned everything there was to know about airplanes. But I did understand how excited I felt when I gazed at the five huge aircrafts that sat on the ground behind the school. The planes were painted a vivid golden color that sparkled brightly in the sun. To add to the excitement, my father would point to planes passing overhead on their way into or out of New York City. Now I realize that those were not just special moments that I shared with my father; they were moments that foreshadowed my future.

I will never forget my first plane ride. I was five years old, and my family, which is Muslim, was traveling to Morocco. I remember a pretty brunette in a uniform coming over to my seat and asking me how I was enjoying the flight. I responded with a toothy grin that earned me a big smile and a chuckle. The stewardess reached into a cart and brought out a pencil case that she placed on my tray table. The pencil case had a black background. On the background was a sky-blue jet plane surrounded by an ivory moon and twinkling stars. The jet was smiling broadly and had a speech bubble next to it that said, "Bon Vol," which means "good flight" in French. That pencil case sits in a place of honor on my desk to this day.

Needless to say, I had no doubt which high school I wanted to attend. But I had to apply to Aviation because it is a competitive high school, and many more kids apply to it than get in. My heart was thumping wildly when the letter arrived in the mail, and my hands were shaking as I tore it open. I shouted, "I made it!" as tears of joy slid down my cheeks. Many people told me that I wouldn't be able to handle the work because it was a "man's job." I ignored their warnings and accepted the challenge enthusiastically. I spent the whole summer researching the school and friending anyone on Facebook who went there. I studied the different types of aircraft and memorized the parts of a Boeing 747. Until then, airplanes had been my passion. Now they were my obsession.

My first day of school was exhilarating. I picked out my favorite abaya, which to me is a symbol of self-respect. I wanted to make a self-confident impression on my teachers and my peers. Little did I know that a big surprise awaited me on that first day. Everywhere I looked, as I walked through the halls, I saw posses of guys. It turned out that only 16% of the students in my class were female. But I have never let that gender imbalance intimidate me.

On my very first shop project, I proved that I was as capable as any guy. Aviation has an extremely rigorous science and math program as well as shop classes in which students are required to construct actual parts of an aircraft. For that shop project, each student, working independently, had four months in which to build a component of an aircraft wing known as an *aileron*. By coming to school early on weekdays and going in on Saturdays over the course of more than three months, I was able to complete that project two weeks before it was due. Not only did I earn an A from my instructor, but many of the guys in the class asked me for help finishing their ailerons. With that early success, I completely shattered the myth that the work at Aviation was "too hard for girls." Since then, my motto has been "The Sky's the Limit."

RAYHANA MAAROUF was born in New York, NY. She attended The Young Women's Leadership School of Astoria in Queens, NY, and LIU Pharmacy School in Brooklyn, NY.

"If I could be didactic about just one thing, though I hope to God that limit is never imposed on me, it would be my belief that young people, young women in particular, must commit their experiences to paper, if for no other reason than this: only you will ever have these experiences, and you won't want to have lost them after you go or forget or grow up and get terrible snow boots. But you may also find, as I did, that the sentences become the planks that form a raft that drags you ashore, wet and gasping on a welcome beach."

--LENA DUNHAM--

Made Out of Diamonds

BY ERIN PENNILL, 2008

My boring bath is now over! The moment I have spent my entire life looking forward to has finally sailed in on a wave of newfound sexiness. I step out of the high-rise bathtub, which is an obstacle in itself. Even though I am a seven-year-old young woman, I am still small, though I think I am fat. As my feet land on the slippery pink-pebbled floor, I immediately snatch up the beautiful ninety-nine-cent-store, hand-me-down training bra from two big cousins ago. My femininity is so captivated by its cheap silky-white texture that it might as well be made out of diamonds.

I ignore the chilly air blowing through the open bathroom door. I'd rather be slightly uncomfortable than have to lock the door and risk getting kidnapped and carried away to hell by a ghost. I pull the cloth over my head and push my arms through the straps, simultaneously imagining how realistic playing boyfriend/girlfriend with my pillow is going to be from now on.

ERIN PENNILL was born in Jersey City, NJ, and grew up in Brooklyn, NY. She attended Science Skills Center High School for Science, Technology and the Creative Arts in Brooklyn, NY, and Borough of Manhattan Community College in New York, NY.

Easy-Bake Oven

BY KIANA MARTE, 2017

I woke up to the smell of bacon and eggs and a feeling in the air I could not quite understand. I didn't have the words back then. Today? I know exactly what it was: tension. I put on my SpongeBob slippers and investigated. Every day was something new, but it wasn't *exciting*, it was chaos. Random, sporadic, and never-ending. I walked through the narrow, gray hallway with my doodles on the wall. I knew my family could hear my steps because the air got lighter. I saw my grandparents and my cousins in the living room with their smiles high but their eyes droopy and their hands clenched. I knew something was wrong, but they wouldn't tell me . . . like always. "I can't believe we're getting kicked out and Mom isn't even here to help us move," my sister said, rolling her eyes. My grandma— we called her *Mama*—gave my sister the evil eye, like she had blurted out a secret. I didn't know what eviction was, but I knew whose fault it was: my mother's. I was used to my mother going on extravagant trips and never taking us. I created my own life and detached myself from reality. My secret home was with my toys. There was one toy that gave me the biggest sense of warmth, no pun intended: the Easy-Bake Oven. A pink plastic rectangle, one little shelf, and the magical ability to bake cookies, cupcakes, and pretzels at any time! My dad gave it to me. He knew I was going to be the best chef in the United States. And I was. I was a tiny, all-powerful chef. I didn't see my dad a lot, but through the Easy-Bake Oven, we could connect from miles away. I was the one creating a masterpiece every day, the one who called the shots. No one could take that away from me.

That morning, the living room was stacked high with cardboard boxes that reminded me of the signs homeless people used to beg with. My eyebrows furrowed at the fact that my Easy-Bake Oven looked like a piece of garbage. I snatched it up, away from the boxes, and held it close. I watched my cousins help Mama tirelessly go up and down the stairs, emptying the bedrooms. She was looking after us all, but she looked like she needed looking after herself. I wish we could have shared the power of the Easy-Bake Oven, but she would probably just end up cleaning it.

I didn't care about the house; home is where the heart is, right? So that meant home was in Puerto Rico, with my mom. My sister was mad that she wasn't here in Brooklyn, taking care of us, stopping those guys from taping up our door. But my sister was wrong, as always. Even if our mom were there, she wouldn't help. She would just sit in the living room awake for hours, scared of the aliens. I was only six, but even I knew there were no aliens. And as for the "people in her head," they were useless; I bet they wouldn't even help us move!

Mama stood, surveying all of the boxes. *"Aye mis niñas, hay demasiados juguetes. Necesito vender esas cosas."* She called it there and then—a yard sale. And it turned out a lot of people were happy to buy our junk. Mama was happy; she told me and my sister to go settle in at her place five blocks away and put some of my clothes away in our new room. I put my Easy-Bake Oven down and told my cousin to keep it safe. I walked through the neighborhood with my sister, into my grandparents' building with the elevator that reeked of pee. I looked at our room; Mama had put sheets on the bed, and that felt good. My sister and I unpacked our plastic bags and stacked the clothes in the drawers, then we took the stairs down, counting as we went. 218! The yard sale was winding down when we reached our old building. I skipped up to my cousin, but she was looking at the ground as if she'd broken her neck.

I knew immediately what had happened. They'd sold my Easy-Bake Oven, and there was nothing I could do about it. I knocked over the ugly lamp sitting on the table in the yard and Mama yelled at me to pick it up. The thing is, I wasn't even mad at her. Or my mom. It crystallized for me right there and then. None of this would have happened, us losing the house, my sister being sad, my dad living miles away, my grandparents selling my toys, if it weren't for my mom's illness. Whatever was up with her got to us all. Losing my Easy-Bake Oven meant losing more than a toy. I lost the child in me. I didn't yet know what I was becoming: a young woman ready to speak up about mental illness.

KIANA MARTE was born in Brooklyn, NY. She attended Cathedral High School in New York, NY, and Binghamton University in Binghamton, NY.

What's Twenty Percent of Forty-Eight?

BY IREEN HOSSAIN, 2011

I had to pee, like really badly, resulting in me waking up. It was dark, and I looked at the bright digital clock, which said 1:32 AM. I got up and headed for the bathroom. The bathroom light was on, meaning someone was in there. I knocked on the door.

The familiar voice of my dad said, "I'm in here."

"Hurry up, Baba! I need to pee!"

"Okay, hold on." In a matter of minutes, my dad came out and I rushed in before my bladder exploded. After I came back out, I saw my dad in the kitchen, looking through the refrigerator.

"There's nothing to eat in here. What did your mom make for dinner?" my dad asked.

"Fried chicken. Why are you home so early?" My dad's a Yellow Cab driver, and he worked the night shifts, coming home at dawn.

"There's no business tonight. Ugh, I'm so hungry," my dad groaned. He walked toward the door. "Go back to bed, I'm going to eat out and then come home."

"I want to eat something too!" I exclaimed.

"Shhh!" my dad shushed me. "You're going to wake your sister up. And no, go to bed, Ireen."

"Please, Baba! I want to go with you!"

My dad rolled his eyes and said, "Fine. But you have to be quiet!" I nodded insanely, like a bobble-head doll. My dad ushered me out of our small apartment.

We went down the eight million stairs from the fourth floor to the first floor and headed outside toward our bluish Toyota van. My dad unlocked the car, and I sat up front next to him. "Where are we going, Baba?"

"You'll see," he said with a smile, and started the car.

We head toward Manhattan from Queens, and then I asked again, "Where are we going?" My dad ignored me. For about fifteen minutes we just hung out in the car, listening to the radio. I was singing along to a song when my dad started to slow down the car. I looked out the window and saw a *long* line of people standing. "Baba, what are they doing?"

My dad proudly said, "They're waiting on line to eat one of the best halal chicken-and-rice platters of New York!" I looked at him a bit confused. "You'll understand when you eat it. Now get out of the car and wait on line. I'm going to park the car."

I did as I was told, and waited on the longest line in history. I had been standing patiently for about ten minutes when my dad finally came and stood next to me. "This is ridiculous, Baba," I told him.

He shook his head. "No, Ireen, the taste of this food is ridiculously good!" I rolled my eyes; he was being so dramatic. "So, how was school today?" my dad asked, trying to make small talk.

"I got the highest grade in my class for English," I bragged.

"What about math and science?"

I glared at him. "Who cares about those classes? I'm going to become a famous writer."

"Life requires math and science! What's twenty percent of forty-eight?"

"Ugh," I groaned. "I don't know!"

"What do you mean you don't know? Its basic knowledge!" my dad exclaimed. "I'm a dump, and now you're being a dump."

"Baba, it's *dumb*."

"Don't correct me! I've been in this country for over ten years, I know my English!"

"Then use it properly!" I exclaimed.

"Don't be smart with me!"

My god, my dad's such a drama king. "I'm not being smart with you, Baba. I'm just telling you that the word is *dumb*, not *dump*."

"Ireen," my dad started on his rant, "even though I dropped out of school, I studied English in Bangladesh, and I got the highest grades."

"Okay, that's great," I told him sarcastically.

"If I went to college, then I could have been a doctor or a businessman. But I didn't listen to my parents. Math and science are very important, and I realized it too late. I don't want you to end up like me."

"Oh my god," I said, and sighed. "I'm sorry, Baba, but you've been stuck with a daughter who's illiterate in math and science."

"What meat do you want?" the gyro man asked. Wow, I didn't even realize we had gotten to the front.

"A mix of beef and chicken, please," my dad said. I watched the gyro man as he prepared the rice platter. The smell was *so* good!

My dad paid the gyro man, and we headed to our car. The moment we got into the car, my dad and I dived into the food. My dad was right; the food was ridiculously good!

The rice mixed with the little pieces of beef and chicken tasted great together. I took out the small container filled with white sauce and put it all over my rice. I combined the rice, meat, and the creamy white sauce. Oh god, the taste was *sensational*.

As my dad was eating he said to me, "If you're going to be a writer then you will be a fantastic writer! Even though you are a dump at math."

I shook my head and grinned. "You mean dumb."

"Don't start with me, Ireen."

IREEN HOSSAIN was born in Bangladesh. She attended The Young Women's Leadership School of Astoria in Queens, NY, and SUNY Plattsburgh in Plattsburgh, NY.

Why Obsessions Matter

BY DIAMOND ABREU, 2017

I never knew that I would be obsessed with comics. When I was ten, I loved playing with dolls and watching Barbie movies. But one day, when my father suggested I watch an action movie with him, there was just something about the speed of the movie and the way it had my heart thumping that caught my attention and never let go. Watching action movies became a ritual for me and my dad, and seeing *Batman: The Dark Knight* was the most memorable moment of all. I liked Batman because he was full of convictions, emotions, and even flaws, whereas other superheroes tend to be practically flawless. I also appreciated how Batman's world paralleled ours but was much darker.

I wanted to find out more about this world and soon realized a whole universe existed in the form of comic books. I felt a sort of excitement build up in my chest as I surfed the internet for local comic book stores on my bulky laptop. I remember tearing/ripping a messy sheet of paper from my notebook to write down the locations. It was Saturday by the time I worked up my courage to tell my dad to drive me there. I remember feeling butterflies because I didn't know what to expect once I got there—I mean, I had never been in a comic book store before.

My fears were unfounded as soon as I entered and immediately noticed how quiet and calm the store was. The sun poured in from the windows, making the comics that were tucked away in plastic covers glimmer. I know I must have looked confused because an employee, who would later become a close friend, came up to ask what I was looking for. When I asked to see Batman comics, he calmly brought me over to a section that was entirely dedicated to them. My eyes immediately widened. The colorful images, big words, and perfectly drawn characters made my heart thump with excitement. I wanted to read as much as I possibly could, so from then on, every Friday after school, I went to the comic book store to check out new issues. You could say that I basically grew up in the comic book store. Eventually, the workers and I began to develop a close bond based on our love for comics. I became comfortable in that small community of avid comic book lovers. Now when the employees see me, I get more than just a robotic "Hello, welcome," but a loud "Hello, Diamond!" accompanied by a warm hug.

My love for comics is fueled by these friendships but also by the colorful worlds and compelling story lines of comic books, which transport me to a whole new world. From eighth grade to my senior year of high school, the comic book store has always been there for me. It served as a sanctuary where I could release everyday stress by escaping into the world of moving images. Without the comic book store, I wouldn't be who I am today. I wouldn't be as bubbly as I am now, since my shyness slips away whenever I talk about comic books. Without comic books, I wouldn't know how to effectively create intriguing characters who have emotions and flaws but are heroes at the same time. The comic book store remains a place where I can be the purest form of myself, and because of that, it will always be a part of my life.

DIAMOND ABREU was born in New York, NY. She attended Millennium High School in New York, NY.

Invasion of the Germs

BY RASHRI SHAMSUNDAR, 2007

The music boomed through the paper-thin walls. I covered my ears tightly and squeezed my eyes shut to drown out the noise. In the dark closet, I tried to hide from the sounds. Memories came flooding back of the consequences from listening to music that was way too loud. The countless times, on the verge of tears, I ran begging Mom to make the pounding, trobulating pain go away; the undesirable visits to the small, bald man who invaded my ears; the unwanted warnings not to eat yumilicious foods such as chocolate or ice cream; the yucky-thick, bubblegum-pink antibiotics; worse yet, the dreaded fear that I would lose my hearing.

First it started with cruelsome earaches. Then it was thin, clear fluid that drip-dropped from my ear. When the fluid became blood, Mom knew it was time to see a doctor. I didn't worry, I was strong, I never cried. The pain was so awful, I would wake in the middle of a deep sleep, crazy from such traumatic, acute throbbing. I could feel and hear the pounding pain; it seemed to sing along with my heartbeat. At six, I couldn't see why these things were happening to me. It wasn't happening to anyone else I knew. I felt as though I was the only person in the universe with an ear infection. Especially when I was at school, none of my friends or classmates had bleeding ears.

My best friend at the time, Miriam, would always whisper "there's red in your ear" whenever she noticed. The random bleeding occurred in the middle of my classes, sometimes even more than once in a day. She would kindly help me get napkins to contain the mess pouring out of me. I had to hold the tissue to my ear, replacing it every few minutes because the fluid was quickly absorbed by these thin papers. One ear bled at a time but there was no telling which it would be. I never felt uncomfortable when I had an accident. Miriam never made a big deal out of the gruesome images of my infection. It was almost like she understood, kind of like she felt what I was going through. It helped me discard any ridicule from the ignorant children.

I didn't even acknowledge the reaction from the other children at school. Whenever my ears started to leak, the kids would pull away. The thick, dark-red blood drooled out of my ear so slowly, I never felt it escape from my ear before their faces scrunched with scorn. Some of their faces even twisted with fear or confusion.

There was one time when my first-grade class was sitting in the lunchroom and my left ear started to bleed. Miriam got me napkins and I quickly accepted her assistance. Lunch had just ended and it was time to go back to the classroom. None of the other kids stood next to me. It was like I had a contagious disease; when my ears bled, my friends were suddenly afraid to stand next to me. But I never cared because I knew it was not something I could control, and I liked the attention from my teachers. I liked knowing that my teachers cared enough to help me out; I was always excused when my ear infection flared. They always spoke to me in a kind, soft voice asking: "Are you in any pain, do you want to go home?" However, it did not overcome the pain.

I grew tired of the infection. "When is it going to stop?" I'd ask my mom. "When you take all your medication and follow all of the doctor's rules," she responded. At home, my siblings would call me deaf because I spoke loudly. "I AM NOT DEAF!!!" I would scream back at them. They would just laugh and continue being purposefully goofy by making harsh jokes at me, pointing their fingers and mimicking the deaf.

Together, they had somehow condemned me to deafness for life, making me afraid of my condition. They were evil compared to the kids at school. I held my tongue to limit my speaking in hopes that if I didn't speak or speak so loud, my hearing would remain. I clung onto the strands of my hearing in fear that if I didn't, it would fly away from me. Lucky for me, the pain stopped, so did the leaks, and the visits to the doctor. That was also the end of the little pink, strawberry-flavored lollipops.

Mom still told me to be careful with the way I treated my ears, constantly telling me "don't wear those earplugs" because I could trigger another ear infection. Of course, I never listened, blasting the music until I could no longer hear anyone or anything. Now that the infection was gone so was my fear of losing my hearing. I could eat all the ice cream and chocolate I wanted, I didn't have to take any antibiotics, and I could talk as loud as I wanted. Of course, I was punished for taking my health for granted. A few years later, the pains came again. That one morning I suddenly woke from unbearable stinging pain, it hurt worse than a tummy ache. The only thought in my mind was that mom said if it happened again, she was not helping me. This is what I got for being stubborn. Still, I went to mom. She turned me away, but I had learned since my last infection. I was ten now, I knew that some hot water would help soothe, so I took the initiative to take care of my little problem.

I look back on my ear infection and remember how hard it was to deal with them at such a young age. It was too difficult to understand how the infection had begun, which only made me even more frightened. Fortunately, my fear of going deaf was far-fetched, for all I had was a pesky ear infection.

RASHRI SHAMSUNDAR was born in Guyana and grew up in New York, NY. She attended Washington Irving High School and Hunter College in New York, NY.

Empire State

BY BRITTANY BARKER, 2010

Where I live, there is pride bellowing from the rooftops of rusted apartment buildings. Voices melt into the ground with choirs of mute prayers laid across city streets. This is nothing but home to me.

Sometimes I imagine myself a foreigner so I can see how she looks from the outside. I bet New York looks confused, with barbed-wire fences for teeth, a dancing skyline for a smile, and a shattered heart broken into five boroughs.

I bet her tears flow like the Hudson River, her pride stands as tall as skyscrapers, and her personality is as playful as Riverbank State Park.

If I didn't know any better, I'd predict that she is an insomniac, a restless girl who never sleeps, with an "Empire State" of mind and theatrical feet.

A foreigner doesn't know the beauty of her insides like I do. New York is nothing but a home to me.

BRITTANY BARKER was born in Harlem, NY. She attended Hostos Lincoln Academy of Science in Bronx, NY, and Dickinson College in Carlisle, PA.

Moving On

BY RYAN MARINI, 2013

Standing in front of the door to my French classroom on Monday morning was more than nerve-wracking. I'd compare it to that moment when Harry's talking to his family in the Forbidden Forest before he goes to Voldemort to sacrifice himself in *The Deathly Hallows*, but I'm not that dramatic. Usually.

Today's the day I get to go back out into the real world after hiding for two days.

Our friendship had just disappeared, shoved under some large object that I couldn't move on my own, left there to rot.

To be honest, it'd been long overdue.

Friendships are rarely ever equal. There's usually someone who gives more than they should (me), and then there's the person that takes more than they should (her).

For five years, I'd bitten my tongue over a lot of things. I'm not the type of person to hop straight into a confrontation, so for peace's sake, I'd stayed quiet.

Now, I'm kind of the opposite. I stand up for myself a little more than I have to and never let things slide. I'm in a period of learning, settling, and readjusting—figuring myself out is a part of that period.

When she called at three in the morning, crying over her latest breakup, I'd be the one to comfort and soothe her so she could go back to bed. When she whined about her mother and their constant arguing, I'd be the one to agree with everything she said even if I didn't agree. I'd be the one to walk her through the English homework that she could do if she tried a little harder, leaving mine for later because she needed me. When I called her in the middle of the afternoon just to talk, she'd never pick up the phone. "Sorry, I was busy," she'd say, and that'd be the only explanation I got every time. When I complained about the family drama in my house or the Spanish project I had to help my brother with, despite my not knowing a word of the language, she'd cut me off to talk about her problems. When I asked her for help with math homework, which she knew off the top of her head, she'd say she didn't do it and leave me alone to struggle with geometric shapes and the confusing equations that accompanied them.

I had no idea what happened. I had no idea why I was suddenly being avoided at all costs, why all my efforts to fix things were completely ignored.

Then came the trash-talking, the belittling, and the rumor-spreading. In girl-world this is completely common; however, I wasn't exactly part of girl-world. I thought all of that was beneath me, and beneath her— though I was proved wrong about that in the end.

When two people spend five years making a place in the world their own, there are always memories left behind. Our initials carved into a bathroom-stall door with the end of a metal ruler in the tenth grade, the place we'd go to skip geometry on the third floor in the ninth grade— they seemed little back then, but now they seem so large that they're almost suffocating.

I take one, two, three deep breaths. The brass doorknob turns underneath my hand and the wooden door opens.

"Bonjour, Madame," I say a little breathlessly. The class is working on a worksheet, but they all look up when I come in. Madame hands me the worksheet and I walk over to my desk.

Completing the worksheet takes little effort on my part, even with her eyes burning a hole into the back of my neck. She's developed a habit of staring now, as if waiting for me to show a bit of sadness or anger that she would immediately say I'd shown because I was without her. Her stare hasn't left me since I walked into the room and a part of me wants to snap.

It won't be long until I get to go to college and into a new world, one where the broken friendships and drama of high school are long behind me. All I have to do now is wait.

RYAN MARINI was born in New York, NY. Ryan attended The Young Women's Leadership School of Queens in Queens, NY, and Rollins College in Winter Park, FL.

Nagiti-Buitu

BY SUYAPA MARTINEZ, 2009

I was still sleeping soundly when I heard a bang on the door. "Noemie! Levantate." I woke up, startled and confused, and then I realized it was only my grandmother. I got up, still blurry from sleep when I felt a tinge of cold water come over me. "Happy birthday!" she said, and then she hugged me. The first thought that ran through my head was, *What is wrong with this woman?* But at the moment I didn't bother asking; I just wanted her to get rid of the cold from my skin.

My grandmother is eighty-two years old. She was born in Iriona, Honduras, and raised twelve kids and ten grandchildren with my grandfather. And yet she still has the energy to shoot a basket. She always shows my cousins and me that she still has the life of a youngblood. When we do something wrong, she looks at us with her fiery brown eyes and that's when we know not to play around. When we all play basketball, I always have her on my team because no one messes with her and she can shoot. When we get dressed for church, she loves to wear her salt-and-pepper wig, which covers her already salt-and-pepper hair. Her coconut-brown skin is just as comforting as hot chocolate on cold winter evenings.

She was raised in a culture where men ruled and women reaped. This culture that my family is from is called *Garifuna*, which has descendants from different tribes in Africa. Over the years she has shown me how the culture affects me and how it works. She has taught me the dances and traditions. One of her favorite traditions is to have a ritual during my birthday, which includes waking me up, throwing water at me, and giving me my birthday hits with her sandals.

Although she never got a good education, she knows plenty. She knows the difference between lettuce and cabbage, which to this day I still can't figure out. She knows that there are fifty states and she knows how to survive on her own. She was married at the age of sixteen, and when she had her twelve children she made sure they had an education. She's always telling me to think before I act and have compassion for others. When it comes right down to it, she might have wits of steel, but she always has a heart of gold. And although she has her weird moments (e.g., throwing water at me), I will always love her. In the end, I'm proud to be a Garifuna and to be called her granddaughter.

SUYAPA MARTINEZ was born in Honduras and grew up in the Bronx and Brooklyn, NY. She attended School for Legal Studies in New York, NY, and College of Westchester in White Plains, NY.

An Extroverted Introvert

BY SAMANTHA VERDUGO, 2017

We all slump into the cold metal chairs. Finals week always took a toll on us. My friends and I are in the Buffalo Wild Wings in Riverdale, ready to gorge on everything we lay our eyes on. In between bantering, we discuss the latest gossip in our high school—a tale of who cheated on who, and sip on iced tea while we wait for our waitress to arrive.

"Two orders of sweet BBQ, two teriyaki, and one blazin', please." My friend Ana never fails to speak with zest.

The waitress gives her a dubious look. "They're the spiciest wings in our menu and y'all seem a little too young to handle it," she claims with a chuckle.

It only takes an assertive look and a "let's fuck it up" from my friend Kat to convince the waitress.

"Y'all remembered to eat right. You can't eat spicy stuff on an empty stomach," the meticulous planner, Ana, remarks.

My eyes widen. "I only ate a banana for breakfast. My burger will fill me up, plus I'm only going to have one blazin' wing. I'll be fine."

The waitress, a curvy woman with extended arms and straight posture, holds up our food. Our eyes light up with joy as she sets the wings before us. We all take a bite of the blazin', partially wanting to test our limits and partially wanting to get it over with.

"It isn't that bad," my red-faced friend Brian, whose fair skin lights up like a stop sign, says with a wavering smile. "This is a test of your will. This isn't meant to be enjoyed," another friend exclaims.

Half of the group finishes only half of a single blazin' wing, and I am one of them. I twist the cap of my milk bottle open, trying to decide if I need it to finish.

Most people have power songs, but I have powerful flashbacks. The milky way before me brings back vivid memories. I always woke up to the scent of boiling milk in Ecuador. My grandma and I got to know each other over warm milk and her honey-sweet words. With wrinkly hands, my grandma would turn the dial on the stove, and the crescendo of the open flame echoed throughout the halls. She wore her technicolored apron and wobbled over to the silver pot to sift the fresh milk from the residual pieces of creamy blob.

As I walked in, she greeted me with a kiss on the cheek. School was always the motif in my "small talk" conversations with family members. But she had an admirable way with words. She was the kind of woman that turned small talk into big talk. "*Sabes que eres mi orgullo. Pero, tienes que seguir así, no solo para superarte, sino también para mi Anita Lucia.*" She would always tell me to continue working hard, that my efforts would pay off one day, and money would no longer be an issue for my mother and me.

I chug my mini bottle of milk and shove cold celery and carrot sticks into my mouth to ease the spiciness. I am determined to finish this four-centimeter piece of chicken, which contained six fresh habañero peppers (with seeds), five lemon-drop peppers, and eight jalapeños (also with seeds).

Memories rush to my brain once again: the stress of college applications, disagreements between my father and me, all those times calculus made me feel stupid, and the countless college interviews. The ones that made me suck up my shyness and get over the uncomfortable feeling of detailing my life story to a stranger who determined my future. "Own that shit. You need to go up there and tell them why you deserve to go there," Ana had said when I refused to meet my Cornell interviewer at the Cornell Club because I thought it would break my spirits, because I thought I wasn't good enough.

Taking a deep breath, I chug a second bottle of milk and finish my last bite of the blazin' wing. It's the pivotal moment. The burning sensation in my eyes from the spiciness coupled with my memories makes me burst into tears. "I can accomplish anything, dammit," I say in between sniffles.

"If you managed to finish that, then I can do half of what you can in life," Ana jokingly proclaims.

A compliment from the biggest go-getter I've ever met brings a smile to my face—the reassuring feeling left me wanting more. I didn't even touch my burger, to say the least, but I'm sure as hell ready to see what else I can accomplish.

SAMANTHA VERDUGO was born in New York, NY. She attended City College Academy of the Arts and Hunter College in New York, NY.

Taunting Little Jar of Sugar

BY XENA LEYCEA-BRUNO, 2015

On Fridays when I'd come home from school I'd straight away take a shower, eat, and do my homework. I wasn't a goody two-shoes or anything. I rushed to get my homework done because early on Saturday mornings my mom would pick me up to take me to her house in the Bronx.

I grew up in Washington Heights with my adoptive parents, but on the weekends I'd sleep over at my biological mom's house. She'd come up and chat with my mom for about twenty minutes while I scurried around finishing up my packing. I packed enough for a week even though I was only staying until Sunday afternoon.

On our journey to her house I'd usually fall asleep. However, our first pit stop, the deli, is where I'd wake up for my ritual bagel with cream cheese and jelly and an orange juice. Then we'd keep on our way to her house and eat our breakfast in the car.

When we'd get to her house we'd sit on her humongous bed all day and just watch movies. If it wasn't time for lunch but I was hungry we'd get up and make our way to the kitchen where she'd make me a cappuccino. I'd sit at the kitchen table while she worked her magic. There was this clear jar filled to the brim with sugar on the middle of the table. The jar and I would have a staring match. I knew I wasn't allowed to eat sugar but the jar would just beg me to. The longer I stared at it the bigger it seemed to get. While my mom's back was still turned I'd lick my finger, put it in the pot, and eat the sugar. I got two or three licks before she'd turn around, spot me and tell me "If you keep eating that sugar your teeth will rot!" Then she'd go back to making the cappuccino and I'd ever so slowly dip my pruned finger into the jar again praying she wouldn't turn around. Finally, she'd be done.

Sometimes my finger would have little crystals of sugar making their way to my mouth as she plopped my mug of cappuccino and whip cream in front of me. She'd kind of frown at me but then I'd give her a smile knowing it got her every time. I'd polish off my finger and put whip cream on my cappuccino as she set out the cheese and crackers that always came along with this snack.

Now when I order coffee it makes me think back to those Saturdays with my mom. But the cappuccinos at coffee shops don't taste the same. It doesn't taste right until I dump about ten packets of sugar into it. I don't think I'll ever find a cappuccino that tastes as good as the ones my mom would make me.

XENA LEYCEA-BRUNO was born in the Bronx, NY. She attended NYC iSchool and City College of New York in New York, NY.

37th Street

BY FAREENA SAMAD, 2016

I turn to look across 37th Street and there it is: a pretty little dress shop.
I walk up the battered concrete and admire from far away. The sequins
and glitter shine under the bright display lights. I lurk for a few more
moments and contemplate whether or not I should walk in. Mother is
waiting for me; she trusts me to quickly return home.

The pretty little dress shop stands out from the blandness of the rest
of the block. It's brightly lit and neatly arranged. Dresses are gracefully
exhibited throughout the store and behind the display window. The store
looks empty, as if no one was worthy to enter. Except for me; I'm worthy.
Every other shop on the block is dull upon comparison. Murky grey
clouds hover above me, leaving the whole city in a dark, cloudy funk. But
the pretty little dress shop is the pearl among a sea of clams on that
block. I want that pearl.

I stalk the pretty little dress shop for another few seconds. Five dresses
dance in front of me. I see a coral-pink star shirt with a pattern of sequins
flowing from the middle to the end of its legs. I see an endless and infi-
nite *azul* sky glittering in broad daylight. I see an orange tabby cat
watching its reflection, twirling the skirt of its dress to see how it fits. I
see an apparition of the upcoming bewitching hour flashing its

abundance of stars, glowing and twinkling under the somber sun, baffling even to the most knowledgeable scientists on Earth. I see its younger sister, the velvet night, waving to her friends and flashing a quick, secret smile to her crush. Each dress is shamelessly seducing me, begging for me to enter.

Is this how it feels to go window shopping?

I turn away from my treasured boutique and walk toward 7th Avenue. I get lost on my way to the subway station. I try to wipe away the glitter that's swirling in my head. The fleeting faces and the odd items being sold on every sharp corner only add to my creeping melancholia. I pass another dress shop but do not feel the same magnetic force as I did before. Its modern fashion and expensive, classy presence fail to beckon me. It's not my pretty little dress shop.

And so, I make my way home to obey Mother, too much of a punk to go rogue.

FAREENA SAMAD was born in Queens, NY. She attended Hillside Arts and Letters Academy in Jamaica, NY, and Hunter College in New York, NY.

"To write is to bring an inner voice into the outer world, to believe that our thoughts are worth entering the thinking of others, and to make real what has never existed in quite the same way before. What could be a better path to self-value than that?"

--GLORIA STEINEM--

By Grace, through Love

BY GRACE HAN, 2017

Dear Outer Grace,

It's me! Inner Grace! As always, I was writing in our journal the other day and something struck me: for eighteen years, you and I have been put together to spell out Grace Grace Han. You are the English word *Grace*; I am a translation of the Korean word *Grace—Eun Hae*. You are the outer Grace; I am the inner. We look the same when we write out our full name together, but you and I couldn't be more different. You like shopping; I like saving money. You like sleeping; I like being busy.

I recently learned in my calculus class about this special pair of angles called *complementary angles*. They are different angles that come together to make one. Guess who I thought of in that instant?

Us! Grace Grace, or Grace Eunhae—*to-may-to, to-mah-to; po-tay-to, po-tah-to*.

I will admit that we have had our differences in the past. With you being American and I Korean, we sure do have those moments of deep

Socratic contemplation of whether to go for the kimchi or the pasta at
the Thanksgiving dinner table. The thing is, at least we can bring something to the table, and like Dad, why not make the best of both worlds
and have some kimchi-pasta? *Yum.*

As polar opposite as we may be, one thing is for certain: we are both
in loooove with words, to which people often respond, "But you're Asian."
It is what I call a forbidden love affair. I remember we reprimanded ourselves for not living up to the "Asian" standards—the ones telling us to
be a doctor or an engineer. But guess what? Words can heal just as doctors do. After all, it was the loving words of our very own Han family
that healed our battle scars from when we were bullied. And it is with
words I plan to take a stand because, like in engineering, words devise
sentences through the construction, rearrangement, and craft of consonants and vowels. I remember all those sleepless nights we would spend
absorbing and taking apart each word of stories we read. So why apologize for not being the "standard" Asian and being Grace Grace as Grace
as can be?

I remember the first time we shared our dreams with one another—
you know, the ones we still hold onto. It was freshman year. You wanted
to find a pink journal, and I wanted to write in it the stories of society-
defying girls whose designation does not determine their destination,
just like the story of you and I. See? Even from the beginning of our time
here in this mortal coil, we have only added to each other, never
subtracted.

Outer Grace, I have something to admit: I always used to envy you
whenever my name, Eun Hae, was auto-corrected into Eunice. In those
moments, the keyboard clacked against my Korean American pride,
often eliciting thoughts of insecurity and a desire to change my name.
And it continued to be embarrassing for me when teachers could not
pronounce Eun Hae, instead pronouncing it "Oon Hi" or "Ee-un Hey,"
to which I always had the unwanted responsibility to say, "My name is
pronounced Unhye."

But I have changed.

While it has taken me a while to learn, I am left humbled by the fact that, though we have not got it all figured out yet, you need me and I you. My foreign name with your common name, together, is a name that cannot be forgotten: Grace Grace.

With love,

Inner Grace

GRACE HAN was born in Queens, NY. She attended Queens High School for the Sciences at York College in Jamaica, NY, and Vassar College in Poughkeepsie, NY.

The Case of the Ugly Black Shoes

BY VALERIE PEREYRA, 2015

There is a children's song my mother used to sing on nights she came home early. My sister on the top bunk and I on the lower, we'd listen to "Los Pollitos Dicen." This is a rough translation:

The little chicks say *pio, pio, pio*? When they're hungry and when they're cold the mother hen looks for corn and wheat. She feeds them and covers them with warmth under her two wings.

Whenever I heard it, I drifted off into complete serenity, to a place where all was safe and warm. I felt at ease because I could feel the weight of my parents' presence at the end of my bed, their voices guiding me into dreamland. I was *bajo sus alas*.

This was the song I heard the night before their court case. At six years old, I had no idea what was happening nor did I know I would have to leave their protective wings in order to help them.

It was a February morning, bitter cold as it usually was in New York City at this time. I rubbed my eyes, disturbed by the dim lighting in this strange room with long rows of benches.

At the front there was an elevated, large desk. Behind it sat a woman in a billowing black robe with dark, watchful eyes. She oozed a presence of strong authority and terrified me.

Thankfully, I was burrowed between my mama and my dad. His leg moved up and down as the lady lawyer we had met in the lobby talked on and on. I peeked over at my older sister who was listening intently, like she was going to speak. I turned my attention once again to the lady lawyer after my mom squeezed my shoulder, leaving a moist imprint.

"Your honor, this case urges special consideration, for their daughter requires medical treatment. She has been wearing orthopedic shoes for over a year due to a walking disability . . ."

I looked down at the horrible, ugly shoes that graced my feet swinging slightly above the floor: my sworn enemy.

"Would you care to explain how this disability was detected . . ." Boy, would I. It had been a busy day, rushing to keep up with my mom. I had fallen behind when I couldn't hold onto the stroller of the kid she babysat anymore, when she called my name, "*Valerie, ¡apúrate!*"

She finally had to stop because I was a good five feet behind her. She looked at me funny.

"*¿Por qué estás caminando así?*"

Walking like what?

"*¡Como un pato! Stop it.*"

I continued to walk, making sure I was at her side, but she kept giving me a sideways glance, "*Hmm. Ay, no.*"

Did I do something wrong?

"A year ago, the doctor at the clinic reported that her right foot was turning inwards when she walked, therefore orthopedic shoes were required."

"I see, how has this affected her besides the physical aspects?"

Silence. The judge's intense eyes turned to me, "Valerie, will you walk for me please?" I shakily got up, wincing as I heard the steel-toed shoes make that dreadful metallic sound every step I took. I kept my head down as I made my way back.

"Sweetie, what do you feel like when you wear those shoes?"

I felt strange; I hated wearing them in school because I was scared everyone was staring since they were so ugly and weird. I tried everything to get out of wearing them but my mother was relentless when it came to my well-being.

"I don't like how they look. I think the other kids will make fun of me. But I have to wear them because my mom says it will make me better. I won't walk like a duck."

The judge smiled and nodded, understanding.

My parents snuggled me between them once again, giving me small smiles. They knew how hard speaking to the judge was for their little chick.

"After hearing your case, I've come to the decision . . ."

I don't remember the verdict; the big words were beyond my six-year-old mind. The one thing I can never forget was my dad bursting out in tears. I had never seen my dad cry.

That was how it was for my parents for over ten years. They provided their little chicks with food, shelter, and warmth in a country where they were stuck in a perpetual state of fear of losing everything. But we were so lucky: my parents had been granted residency.

I was lucky to have my hen and rooster to block me from this fear with the power of their strong wings. While I didn't know it at the time, walking with those shoes I greatly detested was my way to reciprocate the protection they had shown me. In the end, the case of the ugly shoes was won and they relinquished their fear. From then on, I knew I would never "chicken out" when it came to helping my family.

VALERIE PEREYRA was born in Queens, NY. She attended The Beacon School in New York, NY, and SUNY New Paltz in New Paltz, NY.

Baile De Idiomas

BY SOPHIA CHAN, 2012

I. 나를, Myself, Y 我

I. 안녕하세요, 저는 Sophia 입니다.

I learned English and 中文 together while growing up. As a child, though, I had no interest in languages and had found 中文 school very bothersome. However, I was interested in the 日本の club in middle school and have continued my Japanese studies in the 日本の club at my high school right now. When I saw a few 한국어 dramas, I grew very interested in the 한국어 language and culture. I started studying Korean on my own and I realized mi pasión para estudiar idiomas nuevas and am currently aspiring to learn Français y Italiano as well. Usually people think in one language, but I throw around different dialects, and sometimes languages seem to even be having a conversation in my head. I was never really interested in learning about my background, but now that I find myself so infatuated by a foreign culture, I wonder if I should have some pride for my own. In a way, I feel like I am a connecting point for all of the cultures I have been exposed to, but I don't have a clear standing and am still in the stage of organizing myself.

SOPHIA CHAN was born in New York, NY. She attended NYC Lab School for Collaborative Studies and NYU's Rory Meyers College of Nursing in New York, NY.

Friends, Discrimination, Peace

BY KIMBERLEY GARCIA, 2017

For years, I thought the world was gentle and fair, with no conflicts. From the time I was in elementary school, I lived in a diverse neighborhood in Queens. The area was very peaceful; my neighbors were from different countries and practiced their own religions. The school I went to was diverse, too, but no student was left out. I grew up playing with children who were Muslim; I had classmates who are from South America, and friends of African and Latino descent. Many here in the United States were not always Americans (expect Native Americans). Their families came from around the world and made a life here. Today I see the fear of difference that causes stereotyping and discrimination. My first memory of witnessing such prejudice in the form of Islamophobia occurred when I was just a child.

I was eating breakfast with my little sister and Mom at a restaurant. On a television, a video of the 9/11 attack played. I was too caught up in my own world to notice the cashier's angry face when the story came on. I only caught a few words he muttered: "Terrorist Islam," and "Can't trust Muslim guys."

At that time, I didn't know what those words meant, or even what happened on 9/11. I only knew that, each year, my entire school had a moment of silence. In third grade, my teacher finally told the class what happened that day. I was in shock. The more I learned of the history, the worse I felt. At school, I thought discrimination was long gone. I never saw bullying about religion or race. Yet over the years I began to realize discrimination never truly went away. I have met people of different races, religions, and backgrounds that were kind, intelligent, and hard-working, yet they face discrimination.

One of my friends, Udeme, is from Nigeria. When I first met her, I found her kind, intelligent, and strong. She had an American accent. She told me that in sixth grade, she was put in English as a Second Language (ESL) class. Udeme said she was wary but determined in ESL class; she felt both humiliated and appreciative. She was grateful for aid in learning English but was sometimes envious of kids who didn't have to take it. I was both surprised and impressed when I learned that she worked every single day so she would no longer need to take ESL and so her teachers would treat her as an intelligent student.

Another girl, Jennifer, told me she had been bullied throughout her life for being too tall, too smart, but also for being Muslim. In middle school, her peers bullied her based on stereotypes linking Islam and terrorism. Their taunts often blamed her for 9/11, though she was affected as much as anyone. Jennifer's school had little diversity. Without exposure to people who were different, most of the children thought, "All Muslims are terrorists." These encounters hurt Jennifer, but I see how they made her strong. Thanks to friends like Jennifer and Udeme, I have learned the importance of accepting people for who they are and want to share my experience with friends.

Seeing my friends changing for the better through their struggles inspires me to help people to the best of my abilities, as my parents taught me. Even still, it's not always easy to be accepting the "right" way. I can be pushy when I see someone all alone, and sometimes it makes people uncomfortable. It has been a learning process. In the beginning,

I acted hotheaded and didn't really consider how the other person felt. I lost a friend, Isamel, in sixth grade because I tried to force her to be more open.

I took a different approach with my friend Anica, who emigrated from East Asia. She passed her American citizenship exam when she was in elementary school and learned English, yet she remained shy. I saw how Anica could be nervous to try new things and she only spoke up around her closest friends. I encouraged her to try new things and made sure she never sat alone. Anica told me that, in the beginning, she loved and hated how stubbornly I pushed her, since she just recently moved and thought she was going to have a hard time making friends. I may have made her a bit uncomfortable at times, but she still said she had fun hanging out. My experience with Isamel allowed me to improve my relationships with all my friends. Now, I welcome them without forcing it.

Many people struggle daily because they don't feel welcome here. My friends faced challenges upon entering a hostile environment. They have met people who helped them and also those who didn't. I accept people easily due to my childhood, and I believe everybody is special in different ways. If you just talk to them you'll find you have things in common with them. They're not so different from you after all.

KIMBERLEY GARCIA was born in New York, NY. She attended University Neighborhood High School in New York, NY.

Raw Beauty

BY TIANA ZUNIGA, 2015

I think of beauty as something that should be unique, that defines each person differently. But most people seem to think there's only one definition of beauty. For example, my family's view of beauty is that it means having straight, soft hair. I've been relaxing my hair since I was in fifth grade, and over the years my hair has been suffering from all the chemicals I apply to it. This caused chunks of my hair to fall out.

There was a time that I wanted to control my own hair and leave out the chemicals. I didn't mind that it would mean my hair wouldn't be straight and soft anymore. But my family, especially my aunt, hated nappy hair and always wanted me to perm it. It hurt me and made me think that my family doesn't want me to be the real me. My natural hair is a part of me.

At school, my friends have specific ideas about what's beautiful as well. There's this girl named Lilly in my school who has natural hair that's short and uncombed. People make fun of her constantly. One Friday, a friend of mine drew a picture of a tree and told me that the head of the tree looks like Lilly's hair. This pretty much hurt me because if my friends are that harsh about Lilly's hair in its natural state, what might they say about me? There were times that my hair was the center of my friends' focus. They would ask me, "Tiana why doesn't your hair grow as fast as that girl's?" Don't they know that there are genetic factors behind how fast your hair grows? Hair is every girl's burden. The same goes for looks in general. So, I decided to write about the way I look.

The thing I hate the most about my hair is its slow growth rate. This year I've decided to give it a break from all the constricted ponytails and killer chemicals. I even feed it. When I say feed it, I mean I literally serve it breakfast, which includes egg and coffee. I take a small bowl and mix an egg and coffee together in it. Then when I get into the shower, I pour the yolk all over my hair. It's icy cold. Sadly, I still get zero results.

Still, my hair is my own and it is part of what makes me uniquely me. The thing I love most about my hair is its thickness. I love how I can walk my fingers along what feels like sidewalks running across my scalp. It feels like a pillow that has never been touched, and the volume is bigger than the Empire State Building. Most people want thicker hair, but I already have it. Yet I'd rather have people love me for me instead of my thick head of hair.

When I think of other features, there are things I hate about my legs, but also things I love. I don't like their shape. I feel like a bell when I walk. Then, when someone interacts with me, I jingle. But what I love most about my legs is how cold they feel. I know this sounds weird, but I love cool skin. I love rubbing my feet and I love to bend my legs. Most of all, I love walking with them. Not everyone can walk. I have strong legs that can carry me places.

I love to laugh, but I don't like how big my smile can get when I'm laughing. I look like one of those clowns who haunt you at night. I try to be more of a mime who has no emotion and no smile. But that doesn't work so well. So instead, I try to cover my mouth every time I laugh. It looks as if I have just said a curse word. In other words, I laugh so much that I drown in my own laughter. One time I was even punished for laughing in my seventh-grade science class because I was laughing at a SpongeBob episode. I ended up having to stand up and face the wall in front of the class. But the whole time I was thinking it's good to laugh, and I wasn't sorry.

And besides, even if my smile is big, it's perfect. I used to have braces and I'm not going to lie; they were extremely uncomfortable at times. However, the braces did their job of straightening my teeth and allowing me to smile at things I think are great. Plus, smiles just make you a more positive, more attractive person. Maybe the bigger your smile is, the better.

TIANA ZUNIGA was born in the Bronx, NY. She attended Bronx Center for Science and Mathematics in Bronx, NY, and New York University in New York, NY.

I'm Finally Home

BY MEDELIN CUEVAS, 2016

I remember the smell of palm trees and coconut shavings when I got off the plane in Santiago in the Dominican Republic. It was nine years earlier that my family had decided to create a new chapter in a new country. I never imagined the day I would go back to my people, where I belong.

As we walked out of the airport, I saw my Uncle Carlos (that's his middle name; his first name is very long and very difficult to pronounce). He still had the same white, crooked smile and the same motorcycle I used to ride on.

The first thing I did was hug him tight, leaving teardrops on his shirt. "*Te extrañé mucho*," he said, making me cry even more.

After our long welcome-home hugs, we climbed inside his friend's Jeep. It only had five seats, and we were six in total (including his new wife, Ana, whom he mentioned a lot in his letters). As in any family tradition (or is it my family tradition?), the middle child must sit in the middle seat. But I kind of broke that rule because I wanted to see my house.

As we got ourselves comfy (well, tried), my uncle put an old mixtape he made for my mom, titled "*Mi gente está allá*," in the stereo. The music started playing, and everyone was doing a little dance in the jammed seat—except for me. I was looking at the stars and remembering the times I had before leaving: running after the ducks in my backyard, wearing my grandmother's jewelry and heels to make myself look older, the early mornings when I would wake up before the rooster woke the rest of the family and go to the top of the little mountain near our house just to see my grandfather cut the coconuts off the trees.

Snapping myself back to reality, I noticed all the small metal shacks that looked like parts from the Tin Man in *The Wizard of Oz*. After a couple more metal houses, we finally came to a stop at the white concrete house that was decorated with beautiful tropical flowers. While my uncle was reminding the family about the family rules, I hopped out of the Jeep and admired the house for a few seconds. I smelled the fresh air and told myself, "I'm finally home, where I belong."

MEDELIN CUEVAS was born in Santiago, Dominican Republic. She attended H.E.R.O High in Bronx, NY, and SUNY New Paltz in New Paltz, NY.

Switching Beds

BY RUMER LeGENDRE, 2013

When my sister limped through the doorway of the room we shared, it was clear there was no way she could climb the ladder to her top bunk bed. My parents delivered the news: we would have to switch. Since I'm seven years younger, I'd always slept on the bottom—until the day Erin tore her ACL during a soccer game.

Ascending to the top bunk, the first thing I noticed was how close I was to our old white, wobbly ceiling fan. Anger built up in me as I looked down to see my parents helping Erin get comfortable on the only thing I could lay claim to. Our room was supposed to be shared equally, but it had never been equal. Erin's clothes always found their way to my side of the closet, and her books were always on my shelves. The worst was the door, where big block letters nailed into the wood spelled ERIN. Until I was born, this was her room, and no matter how much I protested, my dad refused to remove her name. That night, I wasn't in the mood to talk, so I faked a yawn and, despite my anger, fell asleep.

For the next few days, before she went to work, my mom woke Erin, helped her out of bed and into the living room, made her a hot breakfast, and ensured that she was comfortable on the sofa. The major change came when my mom said I'd have to take over. I felt as if it were the end of the world, but there was no way I could object. I knew my mom could get fired if she kept arriving to work late.

My mom's routine became mine. I woke an hour and a half before school, rushed down the ladder, and assisted Erin in getting out of bed. I did everything my mom did, but I wasn't loving it. My idea of breakfast was milk and cold cereal. Feeling like a servant, I made sure Erin was comfortable on the couch by propping pillows under her leg and adjusting the cushions. I even had to find a television channel she wanted to watch. Before I grabbed my school bag, I went back into our room, passing the ERIN sign, so I could get her crutches and put them near her. For weeks, each day my resentment grew.

One morning when I woke, I was surprised to see Erin's head right next to my mattress. She was standing, hunched over on her crutches. I was still in a sleep daze; it wasn't until I climbed down the ladder, fully conscious, that I realized my sister had gotten out of bed without help from me. Shocked that she had taken such a bold step and done something on her own, I opened the door to let her walk through to the living room. It was the first sign that she was getting back her independence. And a sign of hope for me.

The next morning, Erin dug out a bright-yellow blouse from the top dresser drawer without my assistance. From then on, each day she did little things, like brushing her hair, doing exercises at night, changing outfits, finding her own station on TV, and getting onto the couch by herself. I never admitted it to her or my parents, but with each new sign of her recovery, my smile grew.

A few weeks after I first saw Erin standing by herself, I had just come out of school and was talking with my friends in the dismissal yard. In the midst of all the conversations, I heard: "Hey, Rumer, isn't that your sister?"

Turning, I spotted Erin across the yard, standing with a cane. As I walked over to her, I thought it was so unreal that she had walked ten blocks to my middle school. Although she'd been making steady progress, she'd never walked outside by herself. "I decided to venture out on my own," she said when I reached her.

A big part of me was glad that of all the places Erin could have chosen, either around the corner or a block from our house, she had decided to walk specifically to my school. For the first time since her accident, I was proud of my sister.

From then on, everything was back to normal except the bed. I didn't ask for the bottom bunk because I knew Erin was making big steps to recovery. And although the bed was upsetting, I wasn't resenting her as much because she wasn't depending on me anymore.

That all happened five years ago, when I was eleven. Just this year, I had to write an essay on someone I admire, and my sister came to mind. She got through a really difficult thing despite my not-so-gracious help. I did eventually get my bed back, and I'm sure it was one of the best days for me, but I can't even remember it. What stands out for me about that time is Erin's strength.

RUMER LeGENDRE was born in New York, NY. She attended NYC iSchool in New York, NY, and City College in New York, NY.

My Search for Comfort

BY PALDON DOLMA, 2014

He sits in that room as if he's in a retreat, barely making his way out of that door. As I sweep each room, I reach his door. I surreptitiously step in, afraid of intruding on his business. He is nowhere in the room. I heave a sigh of relief. I peer over the scrawl in the notebook. I drop my broom and imitate his messy cursive in the notebook. *When I grow up I am going to write like this,* I assure myself. *I really want to learn how to write like this . . . so professional.* After some time of simulating his handwriting on the notebook, I felt satisfied and continued my task.

When I lived in India with my uncle's family, I found no connection with anyone. I had really longed for a person who'd listen and care for me but the search was difficult and unprogressive. My brother was the only one I somehow wanted to connect with, but he was always locked in his own zone, barely coming out of that room. My brother and I went to the same school as my two cousins who I was living with, but they acted as if I was a stranger in school. In the first few days of the school, I'd really wanted the guidance from them, as I was lost and oblivious about everything. My sister (my cousin) would rarely come to seek me. School was the place where we had to act like we had no relations. *Maybe they are ashamed of me since I am like the "FOB" type and such a needless burden*, I had assumed. From second to fourth grade, I gradually found my way in school with my helmet haircut, crimson cheeks, and uneven knee-high socks. Tibet is a frigid place and, due to the cold weather, most Tibetans originally born in Tibet have rosy, crimson cheeks.

In 2007, when my uncle announced that we were going to America to meet his sister and our aunt, I was excited and nervous of what would unfold. After our month-long stay in the Bronx in our aunt's house, my aunt decided that my brother and I would stay with her while my uncle and cousins left for India. In a way, I felt as if my shrunken wings were lifted. I didn't have any hatred toward my uncle's family, but as a thirteen-year-old, I understood what comfort meant and the decision made me feel an impending sense of love and affection that I'd greatly longed for. So, in my aunt's house, my brother and I shared a room, which we still do. During the first few months, we would get into countless fights and we were like two opposing parties finding a way to live and breathe in the same space. I didn't want him near me. His presence was a nuisance. We would battle over almost anything, and he'd say that I wasn't supposed to "big mouth" (direct Tibetan translation) or talk back to elders. Partly it was my fault because I believe I was frenzied over finally being able to express my feelings and thoughts. The bubble in me had burst. However, as some years passed, he grew on me. We became close. He stood by me during my high school triviality, my endless chatter about nonsense things, and my curiosities and infatuations about boys. Now, he has become my best friend, always making sure that I'm on task, keeping up with school and veering off from boys. He is no longer a pest, but a person very dear and important to me. He has grown on me and I hope it's reciprocal.

PALDON DOLMA was born in Tibet. She attended Manhattan Hunter Science High School and Hunter College in New York, NY.

You're (Not Quite) Hired

BY ILANA SCHILLER-WEISS, 2013

It seemed almost too good to be true. The internship coordinator from my school had set me up with a job interview at a school-supply company. The pay? Nine dollars an hour, which seemed like a dream wage. I was incredibly excited at the idea of making money but was even more thrilled by the thought of having my first job. I looked forward to the responsibility, and to telling people that I was a working woman.

The night before the interview, I laid out my clothes—a striped dress shirt, black corduroy pants, and a velvet-like blue blazer—and combed the internet to find more about the company. Oddly, there didn't seem to be a scrap of detail about the job anywhere, but I ignored that tidbit and thought that maybe its website was down. I could barely contain my excitement and had some difficulty getting to sleep.

The next day seemed to drag before I was finally released from the fiery gates of school and hopped onto the uptown 6 train.

I got to the site of the interview twenty minutes early and waited outside near the building for my mom. (If all went well and I got the job, she wanted to be there for this significant turning point in my life.) I entered the dark brick building and saw two doormen. I walked up and handed them my ID card, told them the name of the man I was supposed to see, and signed in. As I was about to step into the elevator to press the button, one of the doormen said, "Be careful."

"Sorry?" I said.

"Watch out!" he exclaimed. "He scams."

The doors closed before I had time to answer. *Jesus, there must be some serious rivalry there*, I thought. I didn't take his warning to heart, but I did keep it in the back of my mind.

When I got to my floor, the interviewer introduced himself as the leader of the company and proceeded as if he had already hired me, telling me what to do. His instructions had nothing to do with how my internship coordinator had described the job: data entry and working part-time around the office. The job the man went on about seemed to entail selling odd stickers with stay-in-school slogans—a far cry from what I thought it would be.

The whole thing felt weird.

Midway through the interview, the receptionist called me out—my mom had an emergency and I needed to go. I didn't think a family member had died in the last fifteen minutes, so I figured it had something to do with what the doorman had warned me about earlier. As I left, I was surprised that I didn't feel embarrassed. Instead, I felt relief that I could get out of there, due mainly to sheer nervousness.

I departed and the interviewer looked stunned. He stood at the door of the elevator and it was suddenly clear to me that he didn't buy the excuse of a family emergency. He knew exactly what was going on.

As my mom and I walked away briskly, she revealed that she had learned the interviewer had been arrested and was wanted in several states. He was a con artist, tricking high school kids into scamming other people and never paying his hires. I felt shaken but mostly deflated—like a tire that ran over a sharp, rusty nail. I had dreamed that by the end of the day I'd be gainfully employed. Alas, that wasn't the case.

Some people are trustworthy, but how do you know who they are? There is a life lesson in here somewhere, but I haven't yet figured out exactly what it is. I suppose I should have trusted my gut and left the interview on my own initiative when I felt that the job was not right. But I didn't want to seem rude or hurt his feelings; that nice-girl thing is too ingrained in me. Next time I am in a situation like this, which I hope is never, I promise myself that I will be the one who rescues me.

ILANA SCHILLER-WEISS was born in China. She attended School of the Future in New York, NY, and Smith College in Northampton, MA.

Sunday Call

BY TINA GAO, 2009

Such an ordinary Sunday morning! I got up early as usual, washed my face, and ate the breakfast that Grandma prepared for me. I was planning for the day's routine. Finishing my homework while I'm doing laundry is the best way to save time, so I can get to the computer as soon as possible.

After I wrote the last sentence of my essay, I hurried to turn on my computer. It was almost one o'clock and I had to send an e-mail to my friend before two.

"R.r.r.ring . . ." The telephone. I stopped typing and ran to get it.

I took a glance at the number on the display screen. 01186 . . . —a long-distance call, probably from China. I picked it up joyfully; it must be my grandma from Macau. I was eager to hear her talking on and on in her warm voice. Unexpectedly, a man's "hello" came into my ear.

"Hi, who's this?" I asked cautiously.

"Are you Tina?"

"Yeah," I said, still wondering who he was.

"I'm your Uncle Kevin, and . . ."

I had no idea why he was calling. We had rarely talked. He was always sleeping when I went to my grandparents' apartment in Macau.

"How are Grandma and Grandpa?" I asked in my friendliest voice. He hesitated.

"I have something to tell you," he said. "Your grandpa passed away." I froze. I hoped I was just in a dream. I could not believe what I was hearing. Meanwhile my uncle continued, holding back his tears, trying not to let emotion overcome him, speaking in careful Chinese, as if he were making an announcement. "During the night, very peaceful, in the hospital." His telling me the time made it real for me. I couldn't hold back my tears. My nose was sore and my jaw went weak.

"Your grandpa kept saying your name." I squatted down on my heels on the wooden floor of my living room. I could hardly hear my uncle's words. "Everything will be okay." He was trying to console me, looking for words, but my head was ringing and tears blurred my sight.

I said, "Bye, I have to get off the phone." Because I couldn't talk. I lay flat on the floor, looking up at the white ceiling. I tried not to close my eyes, because if I shut my eyes, I would see my grandpa. I would see us going to have dim sum with Grandma every weekend. I would remember the fried rice that he cooked for me.

I would regret that I wasn't with him. "Why couldn't you wait a little bit longer?" I asked him.

I couldn't forget when I was six and he bought me my first bike. Every weekend I went over to his apartment in Taipa—a smaller island off the main Macau Peninsula in China. It wasn't like the center of Macau. There were not many tall buildings, no Portuguese pavement, but there were a lot more peaceful and unoccupied spaces. It was still a small village at that time. The Venetian Macau resort hotel and the Cotai Strip were not even built yet. The building where my grandparents lived didn't have an elevator. Every time I wanted to ride my little neon-pink bike with two extra wheels, Grandpa had to carry it down from the fourth floor. He was a grandpa who gave me unconditional love even though it was sometimes overwhelming. I realized when I grew up that he and my grandma had really wanted a daughter. They never had one, so when I was born I became the precious little girl.

However, Grandpa was a strict coach. Every time I fell on the hard cement sidewalk, I had to stand up again by myself. My denim jumpsuit usually was muddy when I got home. I soon got annoyed with the bike-riding lessons. But Grandpa kept making me practice every time I came to visit him. I knew he really wanted to improve my balance but I got bored. I started to find excuses to avoid the lessons, such as not coming because I had a lot of homework.

Huh, how childish I was.

2006. January 15. It was only a few more days till the Chinese Lunar New Year, a time when we used to eat together in Hoi Kong Restaurant. Starting from that year, I was missing one red envelope and one person who loved me.

TINA GAO was born in China. She attended International High School at Lafayette in Brooklyn, NY; Stony Brook University in Stony Brook, NY; and Brown University in Providence, RI.

Los Regalos de Angelitos

BY EMILY SARITA, 2012

There are 103 people in my family, and most of them live in the Dominican Republic. This Christmas, we realized it had been too long since we had all been together, so my mom, my dad, my sister, and I decided to spend the holiday with our entire family in the Dominican Republic for the first time in six years.

When we landed, we immediately took off our jackets, happy to be away from the temperamental winter of New York. I smiled as the warm air hit my face, and I marveled at the palm trees as they swung back and forth in the breeze.

We had planned to spend time with my dad's family for Christmas Eve at my aunt's house. I adjusted my brightly colored strapless dress and headed toward the back of the house. Tables decorated with red-and-green tablecloths and beautiful silverware filled the room, and I could see the adults huddled around the small bar in the backyard. The food was laid out buffet style; there was pork with a bit of squeezed lemon, rice with black beans, cooked onions, plantains, yuca, and salad—a traditional meal of a Dominican on Christmas. Spanish Christmas songs played in the background as I walked toward the pictures that were posted on the metal railings. Pictures of my aunts, uncles, and cousins from previous Christmases—happy faces as the moment when they unwrapped a gift was captured by a quick flash. As I looked at the photos and the memories we missed from previous Christmases, it made me realize that there were no pictures of my father, my sister, and me, and I felt sad.

More family arrived, and I met cousins I had never even met before. We all started to talk to each other and take photos, and then we were called for dinner. Before people ate dinner, my cousin said a prayer, and her words made me tear because she said that "she was happy all of our family were here together." We ate our food, and I cherished the time I spent with my cousins.

In my family from my father's side, it is a tradition on Christmas to do Secret Santa, but instead of calling it Secret Santa, we call it *Los Regalos de Angelitos*. *Los Regalos de Angelitos* means "gifts from the angels." We were all called to give our presents to our angelitos. The rules were that young children got chocolate, adolescents received apple cider, and adults received wine. My angelito was a man named Cesar, who was a family friend. I was surprised to see that my little cousin, Michelle, had me as her angelito, and I received apple cider. I realized from this experience and all of my adventures in the Dominican Republic that family is really important. The six years we spent apart from our extended family disconnected us from being a part of so many memories. But this Christmas Eve was one that I will never forget, as it was a night filled with laughs, photographs, and an unforgettable meal.

My great-grandmother passed away this month, and I was so grateful to have been able to be with her one last Christmas.

EMILY SARITA was born in Brooklyn, NY. She attended NYC iSchool in New York, NY, and Schenectady County Community College in Schenectady, NY.

Writing Out of My Shell

ZARIAH JENKINS, 2017

My mother says that talent is something that everyone has, even if they can't find it right away. When I was a little girl, I wanted to be a singer, even though I couldn't sing; a dancer, even though I couldn't dance; at one point, I even wanted to be a rapper. Around four years old, I wanted to be known for something, anything. Just the idea of fame excited me. But as an only child growing up in Brooklyn, New York, I was forced to be creative on my own.

I was a very dramatic kid and loved to act like the characters I read about in books. First, my mother enrolled me in drama class. In elementary school, I would participate in all the school plays but my interest for acting quickly died. Then she signed me up for karate class. In the beginning, I considered myself a karate kid and would practice all the moves at home. At school, I used karate to get kids to stop messing with me or not mess with me at all. But after getting my first belt from karate, I knew that it wasn't for me.

I've always had a voice but was too shy to utter anything out loud. Instead, I wrote my words down; it was easier that way. As a kid, I often read fiction. I fell in love with the characters and was amazed by how real they seemed. I realized that with time I could create stories just like the authors' or even better. Whenever I got bored, I wrote my own stories. My mind was always full of ideas; if I ever thought of something good, I had to quickly write it down before it disappeared.

In middle school, my love for writing grew. One of my closest friends always buried her head in her notebook. Her head was tilted to the side and her eyes were concentrated. Sometimes her long, permed hair would fall into her face and she'd brush it away and continue to work. She would often sketch or write stories, and when her hand would cramp, she would place her pen down, crack her knuckles and, continue writing. When the teacher passed by, she'd shove her notebook into a random section in her binder, pretending like she was working the whole time. One day I asked to peek inside. Her notebook pages were filled with drawings and stories that she had written. I admired her artwork and her stories inspired me to create my own. By the end of the year, I had my own notebook full of creativity. Words that I couldn't speak out loud were easier to say on paper. I felt powerful just by having a pen and paper.

Last year, I wrote (and eventually performed) a piece about racism, based on a video I had watched. In the video, young kids of all races were asked to choose between a black and a white doll and were asked which doll was prettier or smarter. Every single kid chose the white doll for its more positive qualities—even the black kids picked the white doll over their own skin color. Watching this made me realize that black girls (especially young ones) need to know that there are people like them out there and there is nothing wrong with being black.

In the past, I usually wouldn't talk about topics like racism out loud, especially in a writing piece that I knew many people were going to hear. The thing I love most about writing is that it helps me speak up about things I wouldn't say out loud. Last year was the year I decided to step out of my comfort zone and let people hear my voice. To this day, I continue to write and voice my opinions freely, not caring about what other people think. At times I'm still shy, but writing has always helped me slowly come out of my shell.

ZARIAH JENKINS was born in Brooklyn, NY. She attended Midwood High School in Brooklyn, NY, and Baruch College in New York, NY

"Rather than always going for the simple or easy explanation, I've found—time and time again—that I've discovered and learned new things when I've scratched at the surface of my own inner conflicts. Do not shy away from your own personal contradictions. Address the conflicting voices within your heart—real truth lies there."

--QUIARA ALEGRÍA HUDES--

A Taste of Duck and Family

BY PRISCILLA GUO, 2011

Outside, the sidewalk is a little crooked. The little pond in the gutter reflects the glow of the restaurant. Laughing oranges hug the bright yellows in the crowd, while dark clothing melts away with the gleam of crabs and the flesh of ducks. Foreign sounds pound the air with the hammer of a foreign tongue. Two tin teapots find a place at the center of our table. I like to be the one to pour tea into everyone's cups. *Dou Zhu*. Pouring tea. It's not without drips on the tablecloth, but it's become my responsibility to make sure everyone's cup is full. Grandma drinks like a turtle while Grandpa swallows gulps of tea down like an ox.

We all drink zhu while we wait, cracking peanuts in a bowl at the middle of the table. I take only a few, saving the emptiness in me to be filled with the main courses. When the food comes, steaming in the air, everyone at the table shares the universal language of taste. The first dish for my family has always been jellyfish. Cold and slithery. It's hard to chew. It is the beginning. We slurp it up and chew a little, but then we swallow.

All the day's problems burrow themselves down our throats and there is no taste. *Ke yi wang ji.* Forgettable. Chatter hums around the table, filling the air. Our stomachs are empty but our mouths are full of the latest gossip and jokes. Waiting is a big part of the dinner. We all wait together for the next course: Mayonnaise Shrimp with Broccoli, Crab Rice, Fried Tofu, and Peking Pork Chops all at once.

In English, the names inspire nothing in me. They are as evocative as dust—dry and meaningless. In Chinese, ah. It is in Chinese that succulent tastes strike my tongue. It is in Chinese that my belly feels warm in the coldest times. The string of sounds in Chinese brings me to the table where my family sits. They all laugh as they chew the tendons of pork chops or dip the tofu in soy sauce. They are all there, waiting for me.

Glowing puddles laugh.

While jellyfish slide away.

Tasting. Family.

PRISCILLA GUO was born in Forest Hills, Queens, NY. She attended Hunter College High School in New York, NY, and Harvard University in Cambridge, MA.

A Woman with Power

BY ROCHELLE SMITH, 2017

I heard the keys jingle as they turned the lock on the door. Quickly I said goodbye to my friend and continued to do my homework. I sat there practically shaking in the wooden chair at the thought of my mother coming in and yelling at me. I kept my ears open to listen for her every action.

I heard her footsteps get closer to the door, and soon the door opened. She looked at me; I looked back at her. She showed me a small smile and asked, "Lots of homework?" I stared at her, confused, as she proceeded to give me a hug and a kiss on the top of my head. "Yeah, it's been quite the load this week," I answered.

My mother sat down on the mattress on the floor where she sleeps and looked up at me. Her makeup was smudged around her eyes. Her eyes were red with exhaustion. She started to take off her shoes, trying to get comfortable from all the walking she did with heels on.

She sat there and asked me about my day, asked about my homework. She started talking to me as if it was a normal afternoon, not one in the morning on a school night.

She talked to me like she had all the time in the world. Her lips moving. Endless chatter entering one ear and filtering out the other. She would smile her biggest grin, then her eyes would water, but nothing would fall. The red tint of her eyes made from the combination of exhaustion and sorrow.

"Rochelle, there's just so much to be done. So many things I have to do. I have to support you guys, your aunt, and your father, and I'm only one woman. There is only so much I can do alone." I simply nodded. She continued to talk.

As she sat there, she looked so amazing—brave and strong—despite her unflattering appearance, her eyeliner smudged around her eyes, the roots of her graying black hair showing. I looked down at her thinking, *she deserves so much more than what she has now.* Seeing her on that mattress on the floor brought tears to my eyes. Tears she should have been crying. Every word she spoke was one of sadness, but still she chose to look at me and smile. She told me everything was okay.

"I'll do whatever I can to help you guys, but please try and help me out a little too, okay?" She phrased it like a question, but her eyes were pleading. With those eyes, she was asking me to share some of her burden. Again, I simply nodded and gave her a small, reassuring smile as if to say, *everything's okay.*

She told me, "everything we're going through is temporary;" she told me, "it is all going to change." After telling me this, she rubbed her forehead, the stress of the whole situation getting to her. The words she spoke were empty, waiting for the truth to be added to them. She said, "soon we will have everything we ever asked for and it is on me to change the life we live."

The invisible pressure of stress was weighing her down; now I could see it. It was so clear to me. At 7:30 every night after work she would run around the house, vacuuming and cleaning up, struggling to keep everything together. Struggling without telling anyone.

She dropped her hands from her forehead. She leaned back on her palms and smiled at the ceiling. There she sat, holding a heavy weight with her bright smile. Even if she looks in the mirror and says, "Man, I look bad today," I would never be able to agree. Every time I see this woman, I see nothing but the unconditional love she shares.

She sat there, doing what mothers do best. She smiled and laughed when times were at their roughest.

ROCHELLE SMITH was born in New York, NY. She attended Vanguard High School in New York, NY.

Better to Be Ken Than Barbie

BY ROSALYN SANTANA, 2016

When I was young—about seven or eight years old—and in elementary school, my mom would dress me and do my hair. I also had tons of Barbie dolls that I never played with unless my neighbor came over and wanted to play. Although I was young, I did feel different. I was more interested in the things my brothers or uncles wore and the things they did. I was comfortable in jeans and sneakers, and I liked simple things. I was not comfortable in skirts or dresses, but I had to deal with them because I was young. Whenever I played with Barbie dolls I was always the Ken doll—or, when we played house, I would play the father. It was what I felt fit me the most. I wanted to be a tomboy, and as I grew older and began to evolve, that is what others began to identify me as.

When I got to junior high school, I was sort of shy and couldn't completely express myself through my clothing. I didn't exactly wear boy clothes, but I wore what was still comfortable for me and what I felt was the closest to what I actually wanted to wear. I used to claim I was bisexual so it would seem "normal" or acceptable. I've dated guys before, but deep down inside I knew I wanted to be the boy in the relationship.

My mom was already aware of the way I was, the tomboyish type. I never really had to "come out" to her because it was pretty obvious. By the end of junior high school, I knew what I was and I didn't care anymore what others would think. I was done beating around the bush. I knew what I was and that I was only attracted to my own. I had evolved within my self-acceptance and I now was able to be who I'd always wanted to be and wasn't going to hide anymore.

For my eighth-grade prom, I did not go in a dress like the other girls. I wore a black button-down shirt, but under I had a red, black, grey, and white striped shirt. I wore corduroy pants with some Nikes that matched my shirt. I walked into my eighth-grade prom very proud. I automatically felt different and stood out because I was the only girl in this type of wear. The point is that I was evolving within myself, and with my self-acceptance.

There are many forms of evolution. I feel like you can evolve into many things in life. But I have evolved within only this part of my life and I plan on continuing to evolve throughout my future. I want to evolve as a writer, I want to evolve my knowledge, I want to evolve as a musician, and more. Now I am in twelfth grade, almost about to graduate high school, so I will be entering a new chapter in my life. It is okay to feel different sometimes, because you never know if that feeling could turn into something good and help inspire others to have self-acceptance. In life you should want to evolve, even if you don't exactly know where it will take you.

ROSALYN SANTANA was born in Brooklyn, NY. She attended Academy for Young Writers in Brooklyn, NY, and Guttman Community College in New York, NY.

Bubbly

BY SHANILLE MARTIN, 2014

The day I came to America was a day like no other. I hadn't seen my dad for a while. Even if I did, I wouldn't remember him. I was just a little kid back then. I remember the lights: blue, black, yellow, green, and orange. I remember thinking never again would I ever see a view like that. When you experience something so great for the first time, it won't be the same when you do it the next. For example, seeing my father after not being around him for a long time. Every other day of being with him wouldn't feel like that one. When we got off the plane, that's when all my nerves kicked in. What if my dad didn't like me? What if we didn't get along? Then I saw him and I was nothing but bubbly. "Bubbly" is a song by Colbie Caillat. She's not really an A-list artist but she's great.

My dad and I aren't really similar when it comes to the things of this world. For example, music. My dad considers what I listen to absolute rubbish; that's something he'd say. You see I listen to One Direction, Florence and the Machine, Imagine Dragons, The Neighbourhood, and a whole bunch of bands my father has probably never heard of. They sing about falling in love, breakups, going after your dreams. While my dad only listens to gospel. Anything that isn't gospel is absolute nonsense that is ruining the minds of my generation. It's not that I don't like gospel, I actually love it. When I listen to gospel, I feel peaceful and calm. It does make me happy. Then when I'm listening to my favorite artist, I'm all over the place. I'll put on a show in my living room. Another thing about my dad and his love for gospel is how he acts when he's hearing or singing it. When my dad sings he moves his arms in the weirdest ways. He looks kind of like a cat pawing at a roll of yarn. I guess we aren't that different with our reactions to great music. It's just that he takes everything to the next level, not just when it comes to music but just everything in general. It's not just how he sings so loud when we're in public and causes me to pretend not to know him. It's those other things, like how angry he gets when there are strands of my hair lying around.

"Butterfly Fly Away" by Miley Cyrus speaks of the perfect father-daughter relationship. My dad doesn't tuck me in. Well I'm fifteen, so. He refuses to drive me anywhere. Take the train or the bus, he'd say. I don't really get upset when he doesn't do these things because I don't do a lot of the things daughters do. We're both learning our place in this father-daughter relationship.

My father hasn't really raised a child up like he had to do with me. Being a parent, I'm sure, is like slowly diffusing a bomb. You say or do the wrong thing and the child explodes. So, I don't blame him. Yes, he does things I don't like but I know he's learning every day.

We just have to learn to connect with each other, through things such as music. My dad doesn't have to like what I listen to, a lot of people don't. We all have our own taste in music. Yet he can find a silver lining. He can try to see the good in what he thinks is bad.

My dad isn't wrong about the influence of music, not completely anyways. Music can influence a person. Music can change the world. It can start a revolution. When my father realizes how much we can connect through music, I bet he'll be bubbly.

SHANILLE MARTIN was born in Kingston, Jamaica. She attended Academy for Young Writers in Brooklyn, NY, and SUNY Purchase in Purchase, NY.

Erasing Race

BY KARLA KIM, 2013

Microaggression. I wish I had known that word sooner.

A classmate I'll call "Susan" turned to me as we walked through the school hallway and said, "Isn't Phoebe really pretty for an Asian?"

I silently seethed, feeling as if someone had peeled away my skin and jabbed at what defined me. It was much later that I learned that what I had just experienced had a name. Microaggression: brief and commonplace, often unintentional, verbal indignities that convey racial bias. I should've known I wasn't being oversensitive.

My school prides itself on being race-blind. You won't hear overt slurs like, "Ching chong ling long!" or "Go back to where you came from!" ricocheting around the corridors of our brick, prison-like building.

We were expected to be mature and open-minded. Anyone who acted otherwise was not a true member of our "enlightened" community. Like my peers, I wanted to be completely unaware of race. I swore skin color would not be a factor in how I viewed others, because I wanted to be accepted by being the most accepting person on earth.

But it wasn't long before I realized race-blindness was impossible in a school with a population of forty-five percent Asian and fifty percent Caucasian students. No one shunned anyone for being different, but I began to notice the large pockets of Asians sitting a room's length away from non-Asians. Sometimes our "race-unaware" school seemed split in two.

Slowly, my ears became increasingly attuned to phrases like, "It's okay, I only 'Asian failed.'" I was ashamed; the corners of my lips curled downward when I overheard, five minutes before class, "Don't worry man, just ask an Asian kid for the math homework."

I wanted to believe that such comments actually proved that our school was race-blind. Maybe we could imply racial bias because we couldn't possibly mean it. But it was difficult to filter any statements—joke or not—related to my skin through the sieve of race unconsciousness.

Determined not to become the target of microaggressive comments, the implications of my ethnicity set up by both society and myself, I steered clear of those pockets of Asians and desperately tried not to align myself with my color. Maybe I wouldn't feel so uncomfortable and race-conscious.

I began to label for myself what was acceptable and what was not, eliminating the little mannerisms and habits that screamed out, "I'm an Asian!"

It was like finally stepping into the light and seeing all the muddied spots on your body, the grime stuck in your nails and the dust in your hair. All you want to do after that is wash it all away before more people notice that you're not normal.

Monitoring my every action to check and evaluate, "Is that too Asian for me to say?" I'd have a ten-second panic attack when I saw someone reaching toward my iPod, afraid they would ignore my Norah Jones playlist and fixate on my collection of Korean pop music.

Yet I refused to tolerate the same hiding from others.

I rolled my eyes when my Asian friend Cady proudly called herself a Twinkie—yellow on the outside and white on the inside. "I'm practically white," she exclaimed with a smirk. I wanted to demand of her, "Why are you white-washing yourself to lose your culture?" Instead, I smiled in agreement.

How could I attack her when I was no different? Like Cady, I longed to easily step outside the boundaries of our race. She and I were doing whatever it took not to be the typical Asian and escape the negative, unspoken labels: over-achieving, politically quiet, stoic, artless, uncreative, calculating, and timid.

I thought erasing any signs of my race would offer me a chance to truly be Karla, just myself.

Seeing my hypocrisy, it became untenable to continue to allow hidden generalizations and my personal bias to define how I view my identity. Though I am the girl who enjoys singing in front of an audience, reading Shakespeare, and avidly watching *Downton Abbey*, I am also the Korean who's been taught not to stare directly into the eyes of an adult, can reel off the names of the most authentic Korean restaurants in Flushing, and who loves to hear the traditional Korean tales of rabbits and their face-washing routines.

I am more than my race but still part of my race. Although I am miles away from being completely comfortable in my own skin, I know I can sit with whomever I want—be it large pockets of Asians or my non-Asian friends. I can pursue whatever I desire and speak only when I want to, without being wary that I seem too immersed in a culture that molds me.

I won't go back to race-blindness; no one should erase race. I'm both Korean and American, and it's okay that I'm still trying to work out how to reconcile the two.

KARLA KIM was born in New York, NY. She attended Hunter College High School in New York, NY, and the University of Pennsylvania in Philadelphia, PA.

Conversations

BY AMY ZHANG, 2015

I am shy. I don't seem like the shy type with my friends because I'm the loud one. But when I talk to someone who doesn't know how I tick, I act like I'm listening while I am melting inside. What if they think I'm boring? What if they're just being polite? Do I look bored? Am I coming off like a crappy person? Am I blinking weird? Should I make eye contact? Wait, how much eye contact? Oh man, they think I'm insane. I unsuccessfully try to hold in the slippery dangerous words. Did that make sense? Why did I even say that? Wow, I don't love myself. This silence is so awkward. I feel it. It's my fault. What is wrong with me? How do I get out of this? That's when I start uncontrollably blushing.

In my mind, I think that I can contribute without turning into Clifford. A red face is a pain in the butt. Oh, you think it's cute, but it's not at all, especially when you're talking about the Holocaust or the meaning behind Frankenstein's creature.

I don't even have the guts to just say "hi" to my crush in the hallway. When I see him in my periphery, I get super interactive with the person I'm talking to or the stuff in my locker or I fast-walk to my next class lickety-split. I am easier to read than a Dr. Seuss book. He'll know by one look. He'll know from something I said that was just too nice. He'll know from my pink cheeks and how I can't keep eye contact.

I remember everything he's ever said to me. Especially that time I ended up taking the subway home with him alone. It was nerve-wracking and exciting at the same time.

Me: This is so awkward.

Wait, did I just say that to him aloud? Wow, what a great start.

Him: Give me something to work with. Football.

Me: Did you see the last game on Sunday? That call on Vick was crap. He didn't even do anything. "Bad sportsmanship" more like "Blind refs."

Him: No, I didn't watch the game.

Michael. *Achievement Hunter.*

Me: So, who's your favorite Achievement Hunter?

Oh god, I can feel the blood rushing to my face. Who called Clifford? Great, the train is coming. At least the conversation is going and he's talking about *Minecraft* now. He's such a nerd. I like it.

Him: Obviously, Ray, and then Michael. Ryan or Jack. Geoff and Gavin are the worst.

Me: But Jack is only good at trial games.

The train is too loud. Oh my gosh, he bent over just to listen to what I have to say. He cares about what I have to say. How many stops until his? Is he going to sit down on those empty seats? He can get off here and catch an express train.

Me: Hey, don't you get off here?

Him: Yeah, but I can take this to the last stop.

He stayed! He's too nice. Wow, what do I talk to him about next?

Me: Words are hard. Gah!

Him: (Laughs)

Yes! I got him to laugh. Am I blinking weird? Am I smiling too much?
Am I blushing already?

Me: I don't think anyone should waste time with stuff that won't matter.

Him: I love wasting time. (Laughs) Sometimes at 12 AM I get up to do
push-ups.

Me: Weren't you late to class one day because you were out jogging?

Him: Let's not talk about that. (Laughs) So what are your favorite football games you have watched?

He wants to know things. About me.

Me: I don't have favorites. I just want a good game to watch.

Him: Me, too.

Me: Your Jets are doing pretty bad this season.

Him: Yeah, but I'll keep rooting for them.

That smile.

Me: This is my stop.

Him: See you, Amy.

Me: Bye!

I'll definitely see you tomorrow. I cannot do conversations. But practice makes perfect, right?

AMY ZHANG was born in New York, NY. She attended Frank Sinatra School of the Arts in Queens, NY, and University at Albany, SUNY in Albany, NY.

Days of Our Lives

BY EVELYN BERRONES, 2011

It was Saturday around 3:00 AM, maybe. I was lying on my bed ready to go to sleep when I heard a gunshot outside. Nothing out of the ordinary, though, so I tried going to sleep, which didn't work out because people outside were making so much noise screaming. I got up from bed, and when I looked out the window, I saw ambulance lights coming from Cromwell Avenue, right down the block from me. I used to hang out there all the time until a few months ago. I was worried and hoped that nobody I knew was involved, but a few minutes later my friend sent me a text saying that Alexis Abreu was the one who'd gotten shot, and that's all anyone knew. So, I went to sleep with that information, just hoping he would recover and be fine. But I woke up to a text saying that he'd died.

Alexis and I went from middle school buddies to saying hi and bye in the streets, then to just looking at each other, and now to my never seeing him again. It's been two months since his death, and I really miss seeing him around, but all that's left are the memories we shared. I met Alexis through my friend Donald. Donald, Alexis, and a few other kids would sneak into my gym period to hang out. Alexis would play basketball unless the gym teacher brought out the baseball equipment; everybody knew Alexis had a passion for baseball and wanted to be in the major leagues when he grew up. He was about my height, five foot three, or maybe a little taller, dark skin, Dominican, with long black hair. And he always wore a baseball cap. Donald and Alexis would throw balls "accidentally" toward me, and I would chase them. Alexis had a ponytail, and that made him an easy catch. That was what we did—bother each other for fun. But after he graduated, we grew apart. I was still in middle school and he was going to high school.

On the morning I learned that Alexis had died, I was still in shock about Juandy Paredes's murder three months earlier. He was stabbed seven times, and unlike Alexis, he didn't make it to the hospital but collapsed on a concrete floor. He was the first person I knew from my neighborhood to die violently and young. I didn't expect any more deaths like this, but then three months later another friend was taken away.

Before these deaths I never really thought about dying, but now I'm worried about it. I knew that Alexis and Juandy spent more time with their friends than their families, and I knew that like all families, theirs argued, and I knew that they had dropped out of school, causing disappointment. At both funerals, though, the families' crying really broke my heart. At some point tears couldn't come out their eyes, and neither mother could even stand up to see her son in his coffin, lifeless.

When people die, they leave a lot of other people heartbroken and destroyed. And I can't help but think what if I died, or what if someone I truly love passed away. If that happened, I would rather have memories of our good times together than regrets about bad moments. Having friends pass away really made an impact on me and my behavior. I appreciate the people I love more than before, and I try to give fewer headaches because nobody lives forever.

EVELYN BERRONES was born in Guayaquil, Ecuador. She attended Hostos Lincoln Academy of Science in Bronx, NY, and the City University of New York in New York, NY.

Salt on Old Wounds

BY SABRINA PERSAUD, 2017

For a long time, it was all about you. Everything I did in my life—from the way I tied my shoes to the way I wore my heart on my sleeve— revolved around you. I didn't realize this until you were gone.

I don't remember much about that house on the corner of 110th Street. The memories are foggy; some good, most bad. The household was always a battle held for two lovers who forgot how to love. My sister and I used to wave white flags for them, hoping they would see each other and surrender. Hoping he would take her hand to dance the way they used to, but it never happened. Instead, my sister and I took cover in our bedroom, holding each other so close it almost blocked the sounds of our family breaking apart.

After that, everything sort of fell to pieces: my happiness, confidence, faith. I was young, I'm still young, but I didn't know the kind of effect losing you would have on me. I was your little girl for a long time, and then I wasn't. You probably don't know, but it was my choice not to speak to you for those three years. Not Mom's, not her family's, not her friends'; it was mine. You only called when you'd had at least three drinks and you liked to cry *a lot*. I think that's where I get it from, you know? You taught me how to wear my heart on my sleeve, but Mom taught me how to shield my heart from the world. Together, you created a child who is both rough at the edges and soft to the touch.

I sort of had a mantra during those years when I blocked you out; I find myself whispering it sometimes. "If you don't believe, he can't hurt you." If I didn't believe that you would get your act together, be the man I always wished you would be, then there would be no room for disappointment. I didn't have faith in you at all. I didn't believe that you'd be a good father, and a part of me didn't want you to be. Old wounds never seem to heal.

It was that night where everything took a turning point. My sister was turning twenty and she deserved a good birthday party. I knew I didn't want to be around you when you were drunk. It would set off something in me, a fear that was at the back of my mind. It made me uncomfortable when you had a drink in your hand. You thought it was okay to cry to me, or stop me from leaving, or hug me when I didn't want you around. I never stopped you even though I wanted to.

The music was loud and the smell of alcohol danced across the room. I was the only one who didn't have a cup in my hand. I knew I could have a sip if I wanted to—maybe it could have calmed my nerves—but the thought made me more anxious. The kitchen was small, too small, and I couldn't seem to find refuge. You were drunk and I was at the edge of a cliff. You were dancing all across the room and I was trying to hide. I didn't want to be around you—not when you were like that. Memories from years ago came to mind. I saw you in the same state in a different setting; at my uncle's house, at the old apartment, in your mother's home, at the other end of the phone. You found your way close to me and I looked down. I avoided eye contact in hopes that I would become invisible. It did not work. You put your arms around me and swayed back and forth. I felt every fiber in my body tense up. I felt my eyebrows crinkle. I felt a shiver run down my spine. You pressed a kiss to my head and I needed to scream. It was all too much: the smell of alcohol, the music, your arms, your words, *you*. You couldn't understand how badly I needed to be away from you. I had to do something; it felt like the earth was closing in on me. So, I pushed you. I stretched out my hand and placed a distance between you and me. It was soft enough to avoid a scene, but strong enough to make you stop. You stepped back and looked at me with your head tilted to the side. I looked you right in your eye and shook my head. *No.*

I don't want to be in a constant battle with that bottle. I shouldn't have to ask you to put the drink down, put our broken relationship first. I was a little girl once and I needed you to be my hero, but that's not the case today. I don't need to be saved, not by you.

SABRINA PERSAUD was born in Queens, NY. She attended Richard R. Green High School of Teaching in New York, NY.

Black Cherry Soda

BY SAMORI COVINGTON, 2014

School is finally over. I walk over to my locker. Locker number 206. *12-2-32* right left right. It's 2:45 PM and I have to meet Brooke at 3 PM. I speed walk out the massive foam-green front door trying to remember to use my muscles to open it. I say "bye" to the security guards, but as usual they just look at me. I walk past Yogurtland thinking about how good frozen strawberry yogurt would taste even in the winter. Every street is white and covered with snow. I cross a red light and now I'm on Third Street. I look up at the trees and I notice how lonely they look without their leaves. I'm meeting Brooke at our usual place, a café called *s'Nice*. I'm just a block away and I can see the brick-stone restaurant on the corner.

I can taste the fizzing black cherry soda that waits for me there, *mhmm*, and picture catching up on the latest gossip and writing about whatever comes to our minds. "I'm almost there," I say to myself, wishing that the snow would stop.

SAMORI COVINGTON was born in New York, NY. She attended Millennium Brooklyn High School in Brooklyn, NY, and Hampton University in Hampton, VA.

Rebellious Streak

BY ELLA CALLAHAN, 2017

"Mom, when did you start smoking?"

"Probably at fourteen, but you must understand—it was a very different time."

At ten, I understood. She told me enough stories from the seventies that I developed a mental film, colored by her nostalgia, played to psychedelic rock. The pride I had in my adopted mom's rebellious spirit was lost on others. I remembered thinking I'd never be so prim as the friend who coughed and swatted her trail of smoke. Yet in the car the smoke wouldn't leave, so I'd prolong my childhood habit of covering my lower face with my sleeve to keep from being nauseated. My father was unaffected. Though smoking had helped his voice acting career, he'd quit long ago. He once told me in his deep timbre, "They changed it. Smells awful now."

Mom's side had the addiction gene. Aunt J smoked until the MS and morphine killed her. Aunt G would bum a cig from Mom but quickly resorted to nicotine gum, and Grandma had to be hypnotized four times to stop. I suggested G's and Grandma's ways to my mom, but she told me it wouldn't work for her, and "Grandma and my father had surpassed the life expectancy for lifestyles like theirs." One night years ago, I cried to

Aunt L. "She stays healthy, she's going to live a long time," L consoled, but I dreamt of losing a mother again.

In eighth grade, my friend and I would talk about life after our parents or entertain plans of running away—she from her siblings and I from the guilt of the growing rift with my mom. After taking care of Grandma, she had little patience during nights I stayed up perfecting delayed assignments. Between lost sleep and lost interest in school, I lost my lunch privileges. Banished to the cafeteria for a week by the new warden on offense of escape, I secluded myself to the science room for months. But for all my fasts and isolation, nirvana didn't come. Somewhere in the gloom, I was struck. In a kitchen drawer between the sea of batteries and rubber bands was the bright-red Marlboro pack. Loud as an ambulance. The ripped plastic cover would be furtive as fingerprints in dust.

I emerged from the Brooklyn Bridge station. Anxiety was asphyxiating me. I hastily pulled one from the Ziploc in my backpack, then hid behind a closed kiosk, feebly striking, then crushing matchsticks. The wind challenged me, but with cupped hand, I carried the flame to the dry, bent cigarette. I drew in, held it until it punched my throat. I was a pathetic hacking sideshow for passersby. The real college smokers chattered feet away.

Fortunately, my parents didn't notice the new girl that walked into the apartment that afternoon. Henceforth, after smoking, I drank Tropicana to mask the stench, which left a sweetly sick ashen aftertaste. Tired of being my own voyeur, I told the person I foolishly wanted to impress the most. So, hooked on the high from smoking with him those afternoons on park benches, it became harder to ignore middle school's deafening crescendo.

If I dove off the deep end that May like my mom said, I spent a summer alone at the bottom of a pool. The virago I'd created for his gaze drowned; I had to introduce a more anemic self to my friend. I confessed smoking. Turns out she experimented too. But we punks were far less adventurous than the new students. One delinquent showed off his new zip lighter by lighting AXE body spray in the back of history class. I got cred from him for my twenty-dollar St. Marks cartilage piercing, but it wasn't enough—I was just another nerd in awe. I would supply. To advertise, I lit up outside during lunch, and, in a day, I got my first customer. My then-stunned coterie later became my only clientele, but that too faded out. It was at night that my friend and I sauntered the streets and picked up still-burning cigarettes. Passed between us, always beginning, never finishing, the thoughts floating in our emptying heads that longed to escape like the billowing smoke that danced into the ether.

One December's night she said, "I think it was just a phase."

"Yeah, I feel like it was for purely aesthetic reasons. See, I'm not addicted, I'm a social smoker. I have to coerce myself into doing this." I looked down at the glowing orange light.

Maybe it's 'cause of my mom posing a mental block, but I couldn't commit for the rest of my life. In this age, we all know the health risks . . . and that these aren't cheap! The kids choosing that huge expenditure kill the frugal indie-boho image they're going for. It pains me to abide by those ad campaigns but to defy them with no great benefit to myself. I'm not counterculture; I'm another twenty-first-century teen parading my overly glamorized self-destruction.

"Are you even inhaling right?"

For my fifteenth birthday I got a peace lily to clear the air with my mom.

When I came clean to her, she said, "You should have charged them more."

ELLA CALLAHAN was born in China. She attended School of the Future in New York, NY.

My Neighborhood

BY MUHUA LI, 2015

It is often said that "a good neighborhood is better than a brother far off." In my hometown, my neighborhood is like my family. It's hard for people who live in big cities to feel this kind of neighborhood-ship. Since I came to New York, it seems that people don't know their neighbors. After three years, I don't know who lives in the house next to mine.

In a traditional Chinese neighborhood, the living communities are divided and have their own names, just like different small villages. In these neighborhoods, there are small supermarkets and stores where the owners provide space and chairs for people to relax and play mahjong and cards together. People that live around this stronghold will see each other often, so that they get to know each other as time passes. During the cool nights in summer, we chat and play games with each other, kids run around and have fun with each other. And it is not hard for new people to join the community, as long as you bring your kid and yourself to the meeting place. Nobody will get nervous and shy to play with a new neighbor.

One thing that can really help people who live in a building to build relationships is to read the water meter. The water meter can show the amount of water one family uses in a month, and how much each house will pay on their own. We need to read the number and calculate the difference. In my community, we need to go to other people's house and read the meter once a month. Every family in this building takes turn doing it. Sounds so interesting, right? After some months, everyone knows who lives in their building and can see each other's homes and families. This is just a simple thing that helps people to get closer to each other.

MUHUA LI was born in China and lived in Queens, NY. She attended Flushing International High School in Queens, NY, and SUNY Stony Brook in Stony Brook, NY.

"To write from the heart is to illuminate one's existence against many kinds of darkness. Young writers are going deep, feeling hard, self-defining what has——as of yet—— no public face. What a refreshment to me as an older writer. To feel what is so true, so real, so liberating in their work. After all, it is the hard-won freedom we gain ourselves that is truly our own."

--ALICE WALKER--

Grilled Cheese

BY KAYLA GLEMAUD, 2017

The butter bubbles and hisses in the red cast-iron skillet. Usually I'm only tall enough to see the underside of the counter and the caged blue flames flickering onto the pan. Now I pull myself up, grabbing onto the edge of the counter to see more. Today is a special day. I'm six and I'm learning to make my favorite food.

"Don't keep the fire on too high," Ma says. "Turn it down."

The gas stove ticks as I adjust the nozzle from ten to two. I hear the football game playing in the living room and Papa yells incoherently, slamming a cup on the table. I can hear him scratch his black, wiry beard.

I take two pieces of white bread and spread the butter carefully.

"Good, now the cheese. Okay, you can put it in the pan."

While I wait for it to cook, I run to my room. I look outside my bedroom window, past the cotton-candy walls and board games stacked miles high, and I see Papa's tomato garden. Papa loved his tomatoes. The bright red fruit hung from skinny green arms and legs firmly rooted in the soil. He'd shoo away the stray cats from playing with the vines and stop the flies from eating the tomatoes' slimy flesh.

Past Papa's garden were houses all lined up in a row. Little shirts and socks hung from the thin-string clotheslines. I never spoke to these people who lived behind my house, but sometimes I saw them come out in straw sandals and sun hats to water their plants or move a lawn chair inside.

"Come back to the kitchen! Get out of your room. The grilled cheese is burning."

I see the soft fog come from my door and I run out. Dark-brown bread sizzles in the skillet, burnt cheese seeping from the sides.

Ma takes the spatula and scoops up the sorry excuse of a sandwich onto a plate. She gives me a butter knife and says, "Here, you can cut it. But be careful. Please." I cut the sandwich into small strips, different sizes and shapes. Ma looks at the plate. "Um okay. Good." I grin proudly as I look at my grilled cheese. I did this myself; it's mine.

I take a couple of pieces and bring them on a plate to Papa. He's sitting slouched in the big brown rocking chair. As I come into the room he takes the cigarette from his lips and crushes the embers into the glass ashtray. His cartoon sketches are crumpled on the floor around him, the nice ones stacked carefully on the coffee table. The top one shows him in the front of a classroom teaching a room full of students, the sign above his head reads: "Hunting 101." He takes off his thin-rimmed glasses and rubs his nose. Papa takes the plate in his warm hands, the palms covered in calluses.

"Wow, this looks great! Is this for me?" I nod shyly. "Wait, did you make this yourself?" I smile with pride and give him a slice of the sandwich.

He eats the piece and crumbs fall into his beard, hiding between the patches of gray and black. *I made that*, I think to myself as I watch him devour my sandwich.

Many grilled cheeses later, Papa left his chair. He left the house. He left this world.

The ashtray was littered with unfinished cigarettes, his sketches sat untouched on the coffee table, football was never on TV anymore. Ma stopped going outside and started crying whenever she saw his pictures or found one of his old socks in the dryer.

The tomato garden turned black and shriveled up. Brown leaves fell to the dirt. Cats and flies littered the garden's graveyard.

Now I stand alone in the kitchen, looking down at the red skillet. The bread is toasted; the cheese is melted. I cut the sandwich in half. I bring the plate to Ma as she sits in the big brown chair.

She is holding a cigarette gingerly between two fingers. She's shaking. Ma looks up at me, her eyes clouded with sorrow. I don't know what to say. I don't know what I can do. I stand there and give her the plate.

When she eats the warm food, the rainstorm stops and the sun shines through her green eyes.

"Thank you," she says. "This is just what I needed."

KAYLA GLEMAUD was born in Brooklyn, NY. She attended Poly Prep Country Day School in Brooklyn, NY, and Connecticut College in New London, CT.

My Father's Home Is My Mother's Prison

BY RAHAT HUDA, 2016

"Your hair is disgusting. Doesn't your mom ever put oil in it? Maybe it would be less frizzy if she took care of it. Pass me the amla oil on the dresser." I handed my paternal grandmother the small bottle and sat by her feet. I listened to her voice, the voice that taught me to read Qur'an when I was six. She told me how much harder she worked for her seven children than my mom did for us. "Your mother just cooks and cleans all day. She doesn't pay attention to you. That's why your hair is like this. When I was younger, I would give my seven children baths in the lake and catch fish for dinner at the same time. Your mother is sick all the time from doing nothing." My dad listened, head down, fiddling with his mother's cane.

My dad started to become my father. Back home, he scolded us for not appreciating everything our mom did for us, but here he was a coward. He let his mother chip away at mine. My grandmother jabbed my mom with hateful words and snide comments. I remembered the stories she told me of her life when she first got married. My father had moved to America and left her at his parents' house. She was treated like one of the servants. They screamed at her and tortured her emotionally. Now, after having escaped their wrath for ten years, she was being forced to face the root of her depression.

After spending half of our trip with my dad's family, we were allowed to go to my mom's brother's house. We watched *Friends* with my cousins there. We talked for hours and hours. We snuck into the kitchen and ate Nutella from the jar. This was the Bangladesh I remembered from ten years ago.

But, of course, my father was angry that we spent so much time with my mother's family. Five days was too long. We should've been at my aunt's house taking care of my grandmother. That was why we came all this way, wasn't it?

My mom spent a lot of time in the guest room to avoid my grandmother's remarks on every aspect of her life—she was too dark, she didn't feed us, she didn't respect my father. I hid out with her, stroking her hair as she waited for the trip to be over. She didn't have family in America, but at least she had peace there.

I took long showers and studied to escape the harassment. I am my mother's daughter, so my father's family hated me just as much as they hated her. Why didn't I dress like this? Why didn't I act like that? Why was I dark like my mom? It didn't matter that my father was their eldest brother. It didn't matter that my father had put them through college. It didn't matter that my father sent them money when we didn't have enough to get by in America.

A few days before we left for Bhola, my dad was unusually moody. Why didn't we call our grandmother "Dadu"? Why didn't we help her shower? Why were we always in the room?

On the ship that took us to Bhola, my father briefly became my dad again. He spoke to my mom and joked around with us. I tried to enjoy my dad's company when he was in a good mood, afraid that it would end as quickly as it came. I was relieved to be away from my grandmother, and maybe it was my imagination, but my dad seemed to be as well. Maybe he was relieved that he didn't have to choose between his mother and us anymore.

When we finally got to Bhola, my sister and I decided to stay at my late maternal grandfather's tin-roofed house with my mom's family. This didn't go over well with my father. He wanted us to spend our entire trip with his family.

My father told us how much better the seated toilets at his house were compared to the at toilets at my uncle's house. He told us he had air conditioning and the electricity never went off; he didn't realize that the Bangladesh I remembered, the Bangladesh I loved, had blackouts and hand fans.

After we got back to Dhaka, we continued staying at my aunt's house, where my grandmother was as cranky as ever.

My mom bought her three dresses she could wear at home.

"These are ugly. Take them back. What a waste of money," I heard my grandmother say to my father, in an audible voice so that my mom could hear her in the next room.

Later, my father went into the guest room and scolded my mom for not having better taste, for spending money recklessly, for never getting anything right. My mom apologized—she was sorry, she didn't know any better, she just wanted to do something nice. In that moment, I began hating my father. This hatred burned in my heart and made me nauseous because I loved him, and because I didn't want to believe that he was a terrible husband and my mom's worst enemy when he was a great dad and my best friend.

My father sighed heavily as we took our seats on the plane. "You're never going to see your grandmother again," he said to me. I tried to seem heartbroken, but I wasn't. I wouldn't have to see her break my mother into pieces. I wouldn't have to be ashamed at my dad's cowardice. I was relieved. But I was also ashamed of myself—I hated the person my father loved the most.

RAHAT HUDA was born in Queens, NY. She attended Stuyvesant High School in New York, NY, and Middlebury College in Middlebury, VT.

Is This America?

BY ESTHER KIM, 2008

My cousin, Hanbaek, wrestled with his swimming cap as he asked in Korean, "*Ee ga suhya deh-nee?*"

I wrinkled my brow and said, "What was that?"

My Korean cousins and I, an awkward thirteen-year-old, splashed around the chlorinated pool of the Lotte Hotel. We were at Jeju Island, where my cousins grew up and where I had spent so many of my childhood summers. Because of my limited Korean and my shyness, I avoided talking to my cousins and instead hung around my sister. We "Americans" had to stick together, after all. Despite the fact that I looked Korean, around my cousins I felt like an alien. Maybe my Asian friends were right when they teased me about being a "Twinkie"—yellow on the outside, white on the inside.

The Lotte Hotel—with its gilded mirrors, air-conditioning, and all-you-can-eat Western-style buffet—was the last place I expected to see my cousins. They looked uncomfortable in their swimming caps and bathing suits. I felt awkward too. I wanted to step into the pool tiles and onto some gritty sand. Take us to the Jeju beach, my heart begged. Take us back four years.

Jeju Island was special. At night, Jeju Island was the whirring electric fan as we tried to sleep in a sweaty heap of blankets. In the morning, it was eating bap at a crowded table and waving hello to toothless grandmas. It was chasing each other up the hill and posing for pictures like Sailor Moon. It was the ocean, raw and salty, that drenched every part of our memories. The sun would greet us as we scrambled out of Uncle's church van. The hot sand sent us running into the waves. And in the waves, we played until our fingers turned pruney, our lips blue.

Jeju Island was the lightheaded joy of childhood. The feeling that you belong. As a thirteen-year-old in Korea, I found this feeling was no longer there. The Korean language was mysterious and strange. The dirt roads had been paved, and Uncle was often too busy to take us to the beach. While it is disappointing to find things have changed, I'm grateful to my cousins for the memories. I remember what it was like to speak Korean fluently and to blend in with the faces; I remember when claiming "I am Korean" was as natural as playing on the beach. As an American-born Korean, I realize I am different from my cousins and other natives. Even so, my spirit draws instinctively to Hanguk, the land of morning calm, the land of my heritage. As hard as it is, I continue to try to bridge two cultures. As Hanbaek wrestled his swimming cap, I glanced at him and asked, "Hey, ever hear of the golfer Michelle Wie?"

ESTHER KIM was born in Long Island, NY. She attended Paul D. Schreiber High School in Port Washington, NY; Wellesley College in Wellesley, MA; and University of Edinburgh in Edinburgh, Scotland.

Yellow Dress

BY RACHEL GARCIA, 2010

It is hot and sticky out. We are all on the stoop of Ebony's house on 103rd Street; traffic on the block is horrible as usual. The cars are backed up all the way down the next two blocks. The drivers look impatient and some are honking their horns. I am drinking a can of Coke. It is so warm out the can is sweating and the soda is heating up quickly. Ebony's daughter is on the sidewalk playing with Cassie. Everyone on the stoop is quiet. They are all thinking to themselves.

Everyone has been acting different lately. I can't blame them. Even I'm different. The world is different. Ebony is gone now; we can no longer hear her "words of wisdom" or watch her dance the way she used to. I'm texting Ashley back, and when I look up I see Shirley looking at pictures of Ebony. Her eyes look glossy as if she is about to start crying. She stops at one picture of Ebony. In the photo, her hair was jet-black, layered, and straightened. She had a big smile on her face—you could see her teeth. She had on a striped black-and-white sweater. It was a V-neck and cut low enough that you could see her tattoo of a smiley face, sticking its tongue out on her chest.

Shirley laughs a little. She is still looking at the picture as she begins to speak: "I remember the time Ebony was going to meet up with me and we were going to go to a club. She had on this bright-yellow dress. She looked excited, and she thought she looked hot. I asked her what was up with the dress. She said it was new and asked me if I liked it. I told her, you can't be serious—it looks like a curtain. She adjusted the top of the dress and said, well, this dress wasn't cheap and I really like it, I don't care what you think. She went out with her curtain, looking, acting like she was hot stuff, and we had a great time." Everyone laughs. I sit back and picture Ebony walking around with her head held high, the way she always walked. What I wouldn't I give to see Ebony in that yellow dress.

RACHEL GARCIA was born in Queens, NY. She attended the Institute for Collaborative Education in New York, NY.

Warm Milk

BY GIA DEETON, 2017

My mom and I walked in silence under the yellow glow of the polluted night sky. When we reached the door, she handed me the overnight bag that she carried for me while I carried my backpack for school the next day. Before ringing the doorbell, she hugged me and murmured, "I love you. Thanks for being strong. Bea will be okay."

I knew that my older sister, Bea, would not be okay. "I know." I lied. I climbed through the monochromatic stairwell to meet our family friend, Vivien, at her fourth-floor apartment. I was met with a hug and consoling words, while the sound of her teenage son angelically playing piano spilled out of the other room.

The orderliness of Vivien's house was something I'd always admired, but I noticed it even more at that particular time. While my face stung from tears and my arms and nose ached from bruises, I thought about how nicely her marble coasters were stacked. She heated a mug of warm milk, placed it in front of me, and made herself a cup of tea. She sat across from me, her eyes limpid with empathy.

I hadn't forgotten about the discord I'd just witnessed in my own home, and I was thankful for the peaceful atmosphere that surrounded me while I sipped the comforting beverage. Vivien broke the silence and said, "I used to study psychology. I had an uncle who was a lot like Bea, and I was inspired to help people like him. But the first time that I went into the psych ward? I switched majors the next day. It's not a good reality."

I knew that it wasn't a good reality. I knew it the first time it happened, and the second time, and the third time. But this time, the fourth time, was the first time I'd been hit. The first time I saw my mom get kicked in the shins. The first time I took a punch to the face when my sister's mania had spun out of control. And where was my dad, the only person in the household who was physically strong enough to hold her back?

He was out parking the car.

The car (which was filled to the brim with Bea's cigarette butts) that he had used to rush up to her college, bring her back to the city, and drop her off at our house so the school faculty would never suspect that she has bipolar disorder.

I love my parents, but my sister was sick. They should've called the ambulance that night.

Once my dad returned, my parents did everything they could to "restore" Bea so they could send her back to school and avoid another hospital bill, even if it meant neglecting me. I finished the cup of warm milk and excused myself to get ready to take a shower.

The shower had a luxurious setup which included a steamer and two high-pressure showerheads. I stood under the scalding water with enough steam drifting through the room to envelop my entire body. It even concealed my black-and-blue arms and legs, which I would've forgotten about if they weren't causing me so much pain.

I thought about going to school tomorrow. I thought about telling the guidance counselor. Mostly, I thought about how I would act like nothing happened. Early the next morning, I woke up to rays of light gleaming through the window. It wasn't time for school yet, but the apartment was coming to life. I made the bed, taking the time to flatten out all the wrinkles. It was the least I could do to show how grateful I was that I got to sleep at all that night. I wandered out to the kitchen island where Yuri was putting cream cheese on a bagel and Vivien was sipping coffee. A place was set next to her, and when I approached it, I noticed the bowl of Cheerios topped with strawberries.

"Good morning," she chirped. "Would you like cold or warm milk in your cereal?"

Warm milk in cereal? I'd never heard of anyone doing that before, but I knew it was exactly what I needed.

"Warm milk would be great!" I replied.

Yuri wrapped the cream cheese bagel in tinfoil and placed it in a deluxe Ziploc bag that already contained a granola bar and an apple.

"Good morning, I made you a lunch for school," he said.

"Thanks so much!" I set the bag aside to put in my backpack.

Vivien poured the microwaved milk into the bowl and sat down beside me while I ate. My anxiety about the day was soothed a little bit more with each spoonful of Cheerios. My parents couldn't be there for me, but they loved me enough to put me in such good hands. I worried about their safety and my sister's mental health, but it was out of my power to fix my deteriorating family. I knew that I would get through it, and at Vivien's house, I was safe. I ate my Cheerios in peace.

GIA DEETON was born in New York, NY. She attended Baruch College Campus High School in New York, NY, and Stony Brook University in Stony Brook, NY.

My Brother's Name Is Ramon

BY YOLANDRI VARGAS, 2009

My older brother's name is Ramon. He's quite the dancer at any party. My mom and Ramon dance a few times around the living room when something Spanish is on the stereo, which my brother convinced her to buy. That's another thing: my brother is very good at being persuasive.

When we were about three or four years of age, we played together but we never had a bond. In a typical day, we never said as much as five sentences to each other unless we were arguing. Last summer, when he was sixteen, Children's Arts and Science Workshop took my brother out for a trip when I needed him the most, while my mother was in the hospital. The only person I felt like calling was my brother, not my father nor my godmother. And I did get hold of him, but not until the day my mom was due home. The next day my brother was home and everything was back to normal.

My best friend Celia told me a few days later that when she called the house my brother picked up. Before he went to find me, he told Celia, "Thanks for taking care of my sister." I remember laughing so hard when she first told me because it certainly didn't sound like something Ramon would tell her. Now instead of laughing, I tear up. That's when I realized that the light in my brother's eyes is my mother and that my mother means the world to me. I always thought I was self-sufficient, but I learned I'm not, because more than anything I needed my brother right by my side. Without money you can't get anywhere, if you don't have a place to stay you're messed up, and if you have no one by your side you lack common sense. The fact that I needed my brother made me think and analyze. Celia told me that the person whom you fight with the most, you need. This helped me realize that beneath his school grades and stupid comments, he has knowledge. I'm thankful that I have a brother who's slightly amazing.

YOLANDRI VARGAS was born in New York, NY. She attended New Design High School in Manhattan, NY; SUNY Purchase in Purchase, NY; and Lehman College in Bronx, NY.

Flying Bullets

BY E. ALFARO, 2012

Years ago, when I was about eight years old, I used to play hide-and-seek on the street with my friends late at night. I knew I was safe because my parents were watching out for me. Things have changed a lot since then. Gangs like the MS-13 and the Mara 18 have become powerful and seem to be even more influential than the government. They can pay off judges to free themselves from jail at the expense of those they rob and kill. They have become the authority now, forcing people to pay money for "protection."

The day that my father yelled for me to duck from gunfire happened during my city's festival month, called *Fiestas Patronales*. Usually this is a time of celebration, but that year I couldn't participate in the festival's biggest event because people had been shot that night and, with the escalating violence, my parents wouldn't let me go. My friends who were allowed to go later told me that the police took a long time to respond to the attacks and that they were afraid the whole time. Ever since then, they kept looking over their shoulders in fear that a shooting would break out again.

That night, and during others around that time, some of the friends I used to play with in my childhood happened to be in the wrong place at the wrong time. They were just innocent kids who were trying to have fun and enjoy a tradition that they had grown up with. But they are now three meters underground. Even the safety of their parents' watchful care couldn't help them.

Gangs did not hit my home immediately. No one from my family had been assassinated or assaulted. Then came the day that my dad received a suspicious call while the rest of us slept. On the phone was a former neighbor who was arrested for assassinating a member of a rival gang. I remember him as a teenager trying to play baseball with a stick and a deflated ball. As an adult, he tattooed his whole face and joined a gang. He was barely recognizable. The day he called, he wanted my dad to send him money. He didn't threaten us, but we knew that was a given.

Our neighbors thought that we were rich because my parents owned a prosperous business, a three-story house, and a car that was not falling apart. We lived a comfortable life, but we did not have money to spare. After that we couldn't go outside without being scared that someone would shoot us just because we refused to give them a quarter. I couldn't even go to my grandma's house around the corner because I was afraid that someone would kidnap or hurt me. My family's lives were not lives anymore. My mom was always really tense and stressed. She would sometimes yell at us just for laughing out loud. My sister and I would worry when my dad had to go to the capital for fear of what could happen to him. We lived in agony in El Salvador. It was an unbearable situation that forced my family to leave our country, our home, and all we knew, and embark on a new journey to the United States. We weren't so much searching for the American dream as we were trying to escape a nightmare.

My life has taken a 180-degree turn ever since we moved here four years ago. I gave up my friends, my family, my house, my school, my own room, my dog, and other things that I once took for granted in order to be safe. Coming to the U.S. did not only mean leaving everything behind, it also meant starting from zero. New silverware, new bed, new house, new everything.

When I arrived here I did not know the language. I didn't know anyone or how to get anywhere. I felt like I was on a different planet. My first day of school was a complete disaster. All the other kids had friends and I didn't. I couldn't even make new friends because I couldn't communicate with them. When I would get out of school I would hesitate on which direction to go, even though my house was only two blocks away.

All I had when I came here was my mom and sister by my side. My dad had to stay behind in El Salvador to sell or save some of our belongings. All I brought with me was a bag full of clothes, a head full of goals, and a heart full of dreams as we began a new life in an empty studio apartment. I was determined to make my dreams come true because I realized that this is the country of opportunities that you seize yourself. So, I started to work hard when the school year began. I would stay up until midnight reading and translating every single word of my history textbook with a dictionary. I would not go to sleep until I understood the lessons my teachers gave me. It was hard work but I did it. I did it because I wanted to be big. I wanted to reach the sky by doing things I would have never have done if I had stayed in my country. I didn't want my dreams to stay packed away in my bag. I wanted them to fly high.

My family in El Salvador now tells me that things haven't changed a lot since I left. There is still crime on the streets and people being killed every day. I constantly worry about them. My cousin, who is like a brother to me, travels to the capital every day to attend university. I don't want him to become another statistic in the death toll. But as much as I agonize about the situation there, I finally feel ready to go back and visit my family, my grandmas, aunts, uncles, cousins, and friends. I miss them a lot. Even though El Salvador is a violent place, it will always be my home.

E. ALFARO was born in Long Island, NY. She attended Flushing International High School in Queens, NY and Lehman College in Bronx, NY.

Halloween

BY FLOR ALTAMIRANO, 2010

The last time I was sitting at this very place, I had an unexpected call from a police officer. Turns out my brother had been caught with a weapon and was arrested with a group of members from his "ex" gang. I thought I was doing my brother good by not letting my parents know about his arrest. Although I kept reconsidering, I finally decided it would be best to keep this a secret from my parents—most importantly, from my mother.

At this point, I didn't know what to do. I couldn't tell my mom, so I just kept responding "no" when she asked if my brother had called, or if I had seen him or knew where he was. The next morning, my mom stormed into my room, crying. She had learned where my brother was from his girlfriend.

My mother was pissed off, and what really upset her was that I had known and not told her, even though she had constantly asked me where my brother was. "I don't know," I had said, over and over again.

What my mom didn't understand was that all along I'd been thinking of her. I knew this would get her so worried that she'd end up going to bed to escape reality. And she did. Even so, she claimed she had a right to know.

That day, my uncle decided to scream at me for the way I dress (in a nutshell: Marilyn Manson meets Gwen Stefani). He mocked my style and said it was a good thing today was Halloween.

Thankfully, there was a knock on the door. My brother walked into the kitchen. "Hey . . ." he greeted my parents. *Donde estabas?* "Where were you?" *No tienes respeto para esta familia?* "Have you no respect for this family?" *Porque estabas en la carcel?* "Why were you in jail?" *Porque no llegaste a la casa temprano?* "Why didn't you come home early?" These questions assaulted him as he pulled out a chair.

I could think only of my own relief. I would no longer have anything to do with this, and my mom might stop being mad at me. I took a deep breath and relaxed as screams came through the wall while my sisters and I calmly watched TV.

Later that night, I got dressed and went out. I called my mother. *Hola mami.* "Hi, Mom."

Que? "What?"

Nos vamos a una fiesta. "We're going to a party."

No se van a ningun lado. "You're not going anywhere."

Since Halloween, things have gotten better at home. My brother says he's no longer in that gang, but you can tell by the beads he wears that he is.

FLOR ALTAMIRANO grew up in Brooklyn, NY. She attended EBC High School for Public Service–Bushwick in Brooklyn, NY, and City College of New York in New York, NY.

Grandma

BY LASHANDA ANAKWAH, 2012

My grandma is in Ghana. The U.S. is no place for her—she needs to wake up and have someone cook for her and have nothing to worry about. Here my grandma babysat and was stressed out. I was sad when I realized she was actually leaving. She came here when I was born, to take care of me. As long as I've been alive she's been here. I haven't called her, not once since she's been gone. It's been a month and a half. I tried once—I really did—but she didn't pick up. My dad has the number and there's a five-hour difference; whenever I remember she would be sleeping.

Grandma. I've always known her to be short and reliable. Quiet and meek mannered. But quietly fierce. Her hushed effectual warnings, "Be a good girl." "Don't hang out with the wrong people."

"All right." Me, nodding my head intently. I've never doubted her wish for me to succeed. The bond we share is held together by time. We shared the same bed when I was younger. She would wake up to wet sheets. Scolding all the way to the bathroom, by the time she returned all was forgiven. She cut the crust of my bread. Spoiled me to the point where—it was just too much. "You treat me like trash!" My way of saying "you're smothering me." My grandma, hurt to her core, reported me to my parents. She told them I said she treats me like garbage. But I hadn't said that at all. I said trash, *trash*. Garbage made it seem so much worse. I had to get on my knees and apologize.

My grandma hates to dance. And whenever my dad talks to her she's submissive. He yells at her, his mother, as if she were *his* child. It's always bothered me.

"A woman should be quiet," my grandma said the next time I visited her house. She had heard me hollering my sister's name when she was over at our house. It's a loud house we live in; we're always screaming. "You shouldn't yell like that." "Okay." Me, always nodding.

My grandma. She lived in the other building. Let me explain. I live in Tracey Towers. It's two huge towers. Connected by a ramp. My grandmother lived in the other tower. "Why don't you come over to visit me?" Silence on my end of the line. I had no real reason on why I hardly visited. She was two minutes away. She always let it go. I was cruel, I know, but I also knew my grandma loved me regardless. I don't understand it. Why couldn't I have visited her more?

Why can't I call her? I beat myself up about it. What if the impossible were to happen? What if I lose my chance forever? What then?

LASHANDA ANAKWAH was born in the Bronx, NY. She attended Marble Hill School for International Studies in Bronx, NY, and Ithaca College in Ithaca, NY.

The Dreams They Carried

BY DIANA ROMERO, 2016

MERCEDES: THE LOST DREAM

952 full moons ago, I was born on a small island in the Caribbean, in an even smaller town in the middle of nowhere. I, Diana Mercedes Santana, was born into the dark era of Trujillo's dictatorship. My father's manipulative mind-set was carved into his DNA by the depraved morals of the republic. He's been corrupted by the ideals of the leaders of this nation, he's strong, and he's strict. I've grown up trying to be the perfect daughter he wants, the perfect daughter he *needs*.

I tell myself that, deep inside, there is still a chance that he loves me. "He just doesn't show it," I try to tell myself. But I am a woman, no longer a little girl. I'm blossoming into the maturity of life and trying to live with purity and innocence—you have to hold on to that for as long as possible in this world. But here, girls like me are a worthless piece of flesh formed under the creation of a man.

I can't dream. Each night is an endless void of darkness. I am not allowed to dream, because I have to work. I have to work hard to earn the value of the sweat on my forehead. But when I do dream, I sing. I imagine serenading the birds and bringing life to the empty fields. I imagine singing to the wind and lifting the heartache in my spirit. But then, without warning everything disappears. And I'm left struggling in the dark. Working.

JOSELYN: THE FALLING DREAM

About 1,290 days ago, God carefully crafted my beautiful self. Born and raised a *Quisqueyano*, I lived a blessed eleven years of my life. In my father's eyes, I was a queen. I meant the world to him, and he was my galaxy. Lepido was the greatest father in the world. I never felt unprivileged or deficient in his eyes, I felt like the richest girl in the world. He named me *Santa* because I was his Saint. Living in a world with only men, having a daughter was a blessing.

My mother . . . she is lost. She has lived my entire childhood with a wall wrapped around her heart; she doesn't let me in, and I don't ponder. She loves me, I know she does, but she loves me in her way. It's been difficult for her, losing every single one of her husbands, including my father.

I was eleven years old when he passed away. It's been years, and the damaged wound keeps getting bigger and the pain getting stronger. I lost everything that night, without even realizing it. I never got to say goodbye. I was covered in dark for an entire year, but I still feel like the veil has yet to be lifted. I miss him. My mom is still lost.

But I dream. I dream I am standing in front of a prominent educational institute, with the founding president by my side. I'm holding my diploma for "Honorable Educator." I am proud. But daydreaming is for confused children. I am a grown adult and I'm struggling to make ends meet in a different culture. I'm afraid my dream of teaching has been lost forever. Now, conformity is my best option.

FRANCHESCA: THE NEW DREAM

I was born in the Dominican Republic just in time to say goodbye to the twentieth century. Whenever people ask me where I come from, I tell them that I come from a warrior. And when they look confused, I tell them my mother was a warrior. She reminds me every day that I need to keep my feet on solid ground and stand up for what I believe in, while never giving up on my dreams. She had a dream once, and it was taken from her. She had to literally pack up her dreams and walk into an entirely distant world, all by herself. And she was never given a second chance. Until I came along.

Before I packed my bags and came to New York, my grandma told me that with God, everything was possible, and that no dream was too big or too abstract to exist in your imagination. She told me she was proud of the girl I was and the woman I will soon become. I am my mom's second chance, just like my mom was Grandma's second chance, even if they never knew it.

Here I am, sixteen years later, realizing that the future is in my hands, that my dreams will not only fulfill my fate but unite our destinies. I dream of writing in the stars, and inspiring those with voices to tell their story and their passions. It's in my hand to rewrite history, one word at a time.

DIANA ROMERO was born in Santiago, Dominican Republic and lived in the Bronx, NY. She attended The Beacon School in New York, NY, and Ithaca College in Ithaca, NY.

In Search of Darker Planets

BY EDEN DIAMOND STATEN, 2017

In a piece for the *New York Times*, Claudia Rankine, a black poet and essayist, wrote that "the condition of black life is one of mourning." If you grew up as a black person in America, you know just how true and sad this statement is. You mourn for lost opportunities, lost futures, and lost histories. You mourn for all that has been denied to you and other people like you. Every black person I have ever met, liberal or conservative, knows to some extent that our history has been one tinged with suffering. Some may try to ignore it, but that shared knowledge still remains. We are reminded of it every day.

Growing up, the concept of racism was not foreign to me in the slightest. Internalized racism had planted its seed from an early age. In kindergarten, I used to squeeze the ends of my fingers until the skin there turned pale and bloodless, and wished for that to be my natural skin color. And I remember when a part of my morning routine involved waking up to updates on the Trayvon Martin case while getting ready for school.

However, it was not until the murder of Michael Brown that I started to truly interrogate the reality of systemic antiblackness in America. I first learned about Brown's death through Tumblr, which was inundated with live streams of protests, articles about the shooting, and criticisms of America's so-called "justice" system. My Facebook was about the same. It was hard not to look away.

One muggy day in the summer of 2014, while at a bus stop, I broached the topic of Brown's death with my grandmother. She was not so much shocked at the circumstances of his death but rather, resigned. I expressed hope for a better, more racially tolerant future, but it felt meager, insufficient. She is a woman who grew up in the Jim Crow-era South; she was beyond surprise at the ways this country can mangle a black body. At that point, the shock was starting to wear off for me as well.

That fall, the grand jury ruled that Darren Wilson would not be indicted for the murder of Brown. In the nights that followed, I thought about how I, as well as my family and friends, could easily become another hashtag, another statistic, another memorial. There I was, at fifteen years old, contemplating how I would react if one of my older brothers had the misfortune of "fitting a description." But what struck me about this case in particular was not just the anger and despair it caused me, or the sheer brutality of it, even. It was that I finally had the words to articulate my fury; I had the power of knowing that there was a common thread between my desire for white skin and Brown's death at the hands of a white police officer. From there, the loosening of that thread could begin.

Since that summer, I have involved myself more in activism.

I have also learned the significance of shared, recognized pain. One of the most profound experiences I have had as an activist was attending a public wake for black women who were victims of state violence. To see such an outpouring of grief for those who are most likely to be pushed aside and forgotten was transformative. I learned how poignant it can be to put a name and face to our grief.

One day, I would like to become a professor and writer. I would like to reach other people like me who live with this anger and malaise they cannot name. I want to work to create a world where young black children never have to wish their skin bloodless in order to feel beautiful. This is a problem with no clear solution, a question with no simple answer. However, there is still meaning in this struggle. It has not been easy, but I must carry on.

EDEN DIAMOND STATEN was born in New York, NY. She attended High School of Art and Design in New York, NY, and Bennington College in Bennington, VT.

Special thanks to all of the girls, mentors, staff, volunteers, and the Board of Directors of the Girls Write Now organization, and to Founder and Executive Director Maya Nussbaum, Director of Special Initiatives Molly MacDermot, Publicist Meg Cassidy, Director of Operations Tracy Steele, Director of Programs Maria Campo, Assistant Director of Programs Naomi Solomon, Program Manager Isabel Abrams, Senior Program Coordinator Sierra Ritz, Development Coordinator Georgia Wei, mentee alumna Natalia Vargas-Caba, and to interns Spencer George, Jasmin Jin, Ellie Maddock, and Victoria Sanchez.

Founded twenty years ago, **GIRLS WRITE NOW** is New York's first and only writing and mentoring organization for girls, and one of the nation's top after-school programs. The writers—90% high-need and 95% girls of color—have performed at Lincoln Center and the United Nations, published original work in *Newsweek*, the *New York Times*, and *BuzzFeed*, and earned hundreds of Scholastic Art & Writing Awards for their anthologies. 100% of Girls Write Now's seniors go to college—more than half with awards and scholarships. Girls Write Now has been featured in *Forbes*, the *Wall Street Journal, NBC Nightly News, ABC Good Morning, Glamour, Elle, Upworthy*, and many others.

www.girlswritenow.org